The Road to
Independent
Reading
and Writing

whole group >

< small group |

| centers >

by Cathy Collier, M.S.Ed.

Publishing Credits

Corinne Burton, M.A.Ed., *Publisher*
Aubrie Nielsen, M.S.Ed., *EVP of Content Development*
Véronique Bos, *Creative Director*
Cathy Hernandez, *Senior Content Manager*
David Slayton, *Assistant Editor*
Robin Erickson, *Art Director*

Consultants

Jodene Lynn Smith, M.A.
Carol Gatewood, M.A.Ed.

Image Credits: pp 23, 25, 29, 63-64, 73, 113, 281–284, 287, Cathy Collier; All other images from iStock and/or Shutterstock.

5482 Argosy Avenue
Huntington Beach, CA 92649-1039
www.tcmpub.com/shell-education
ISBN 978-1-0876-3150-9
© 2022 Shell Educational Publishing, Inc.

Table of Contents

From the Author

I've always known I wanted to be a teacher. On Saturdays, I made my younger brother and sister play school with me. When I was in the fourth grade my dad brought home a box of carbon paper. It was a dream come true! I could make two worksheets at once! My brother and sister did not appreciate my excitement.

Over the years, so many teachers have had great influence on who I am. I LOVED my kindergarten teacher, Mrs. Nelson, even though I can only remember naptime, singing, painting with fat brushes on easels, and the smell of tempera paint. My mom opened all my parent-teacher conferences saying, "I know Cathy talks too much. What else can you tell me?" Yes, that was me.

So no one was surprised when I became a teacher. I taught students with learning disabilities and third grade general education students, but I found my home in the kindergarten classroom. There's nothing like the buzz of kindergartners actively learning and interacting with me, with their classmates, and with manipulatives. I love the light bulbs that go off in early learning and being on the ground floor of someone's educational experience. I am passionate about instilling not only a love of learning, but a confidence in learning.

My most important tips are easy:
1. Be consistent.
2. Be explicit in your lessons and your expectations.
3. Be relentless in your desire to ensure each student succeeds.
4. Be flexible, because sometimes the best plans aren't actually the best for that day or that group of students. It's okay. Find a new way.

I *was* surprised when I discovered I loved teaching teachers just as much as I loved teaching children. When I presented at my first conference, I was hooked. Since then, I have had the privilege of presenting and providing professional development to teachers at districts and conferences across the United States. And now, I am thrilled to share with you what I know about teaching early learners to become independent readers and writers. But I'm not done. I'm always looking for new ways to help students, so stay tuned, and keep in touch.

—Cathy Collier

Twitter: @Wiseowlcathy
Facebook: cathycollierthewiseowl

The Road to
Independent
Writing

Introduction to Writing

When I started teaching, we didn't have a writing curriculum. We were expected to get kindergartners to write, so I did. Well, that isn't exactly true. I had them copy. I had them trace. I had them write their names. Oh, and I taught penmanship. But I didn't have them write.

When I transferred to a new school, I met a powerful principal who made me a better teacher. She expected me to teach writing, and she expected my students to write. Independently. As a matter of fact, she expected them to independently write four sentences on a topic. No excuses. I was determined not to let her down, and I wouldn't let my students down.

What I realized about writing is this: It's all about confidence. In the five years before kindergarten, many children are "taught" just how much they don't know and just how much they can't do. As parents, we think we're being encouraging. When children show us their writing, we say, "Oh, that's a good try. Let me show you how it should *really* look." We say things such as, "That's not how you spell that word," and we create children who are obsessed with "How do you spell?" Then when they come to school, they are quick to say, "I can't do that," or "I can't write." The most important thing we do as teachers is to change that mindset. We have to ensure that children experience some early success and take the fear out of writing. Once the fear is gone, the writing is easy.

That was the beginning of a tool I call the *Sentence Maker.* I created this tool to enable my kindergarten students to write four sentences on a topic independently. We practiced it as a whole group, and then they practiced it individually. You'll learn about the Sentence Maker in this chapter. You'll also see how I taught my students to write independently throughout the day, not just during writing time. I realized they couldn't be expected to write independently by simply being "exposed" to the idea. My writing instruction needed to be explicit and carefully scaffolded.

The first year I was tasked with teaching my students to write four sentences on a topic, 17 of my 18 students were able to accomplish the end-of-year writing test successfully. Since then, I have used the Sentence Maker with excellent results year after year. It's the perfect springboard to writing confidence, writing independence, and writing success.

In this chapter, I share the strategies and routines I used to teach my kindergartners to write. I provide a glimpse into my classroom with the step-by-step lessons that taught my students the skills they needed to write independently. I also show how to create a rich environment with resources and tools that support beginning writers. And I provide a sample time line showing what lessons come first and how learning is scaffolded and reinforced throughout the year.

Writing instruction starts with the whole group. We share the pen from Day 1, meaning that we compose and write everything together. Students gather on the carpet around a sheet of chart paper. At first, they don't have anything in their hands, but they are participating orally and physically using the routines in this book. The basic materials are chart paper, markers (preferably bullet-tipped, so students who come to the easel can easily write with them), and a spacer. I use a 12-inch ruler as a spacer. It's the right size for making large spaces between words on chart paper. Students are taught to stretch words, write letters (including penmanship), and write sight words during these whole-group lessons. This routine starts the first week of kindergarten and continues until midyear. Students also use writing skills, both in shared settings and independently, as they help create anchor charts and content lesson materials.

Midyear, I transition students to independent writing. This begins on the carpet with the whole group. After a few weeks of practice writing in this controlled whole-group setting, students are set free to write independently. They have tools for

Implementing Writing Instruction

writing, and they are allowed to choose their own topics. The *Sentence Maker* (see page 91) is in their writing folders, in their pencil boxes, and at centers. However, as with any tool, when you don't need it, you don't use it. Students are not required to emulate the "scripted" writing the Sentence Maker provides.

Centers are the perfect vehicle for writing practice. I scaffold student learning by controlling the "construct" while changing the content each week. Students are first taught a routine or "construct" in the whole group, and then they use it in centers. As the center content changes, students learn to use the routine or "construct" with the new content.

Whole-Group Writing

Let's take a closer look at the environment for whole-group writing. I use an easel that is eye-level for students when they are sitting on the carpet. I especially love a magnetic easel. Near the easel, I have a sound chart on display. This enables me to make connections to the sound chart throughout the lesson. I use it for beginning and ending sounds and also for short vowel connections (*cat, jet, fish, dog, sun*), long vowel patterns (*gate, leaf, queen, x-ray*), and special vowels (*moon*). We also connect nasals (*ring*) and *r*-controlled vowels (*yarn*). A word wall is in clear view of students and displays word cards with words neatly written or printed with a dark block font. We use the word wall constantly during writing. One student can be sent to the word wall to locate a word and shout it back to the group. We always use word-wall words to write our topic sentences.

Whole-group writing can mean different things to different people. When I use the term, I mean I am sharing the pen with students. They do *most* of the writing. I am there to serve two purposes: guide and explain. I guide the process, from stretching words, to pointing out the need for word-wall words, to saying letter penmanship directions. I explain the reasons some word patterns or vowel sounds are the way they are. Sometimes this isn't easy to explain because the English language is so complex, but I do my best. For example, I'll say, "I think it's one vowel because it has a short vowel sound." Or if we are writing the word *hive*, and we've stretched the first three letters, I might say, "I think I hear a long vowel sound, so it must be a vowel team. This word has a silent *e* at the end, and it makes the *i* say /ī/."

Implementing Writing Instruction *(cont.)*

Here is a list of the materials on hand at the easel:

Chart Paper—I clip a sheet of chart paper to the easel. I have used unlined chart paper and even bulletin board paper as the background. At the beginning of the year, I draw faint pencil lines on the paper before the lesson, so students have a guiding line. I believe they need something to ground their writing or it will be out of control. I think children like boundaries, even when they think they don't.

Glue Stick—This comes in handy when mistakes are made. You can tear off a bottom corner of the chart paper and glue it in place to cover a mistake. It's like editing tape, but it's free.

Bullet-Tip Markers—I have a set of bullet-tip markers at my easel. I choose these markers because chisel-tip markers can create problems for new writers. If they don't hold them the right way, the writing can be wonky. When we start writing, I use a different color for each sentence as a visual cue to designate the different sentences, but that doesn't last long. I do, however, think that writing with different colors for each story helps the stories stand out when you display them on the wall.

Ruler—It's the best spacer I know. It's wide enough for spaces that can be seen by the whole group. I affix two business-card sized magnets on the back so the ruler adheres to the board when placed between words. I also use it as a pointer to reread a sentence once we add each word.

Small Dry-Erase Board and Marker—I always have a small dry-erase board and marker handy for demonstrating letter formation. I can write a letter or word on the dry-erase board, and the student can write it on the chart paper.

Penmanship Directions—I use very specific language when giving directions (pages 20–21) for writing each letter. I say the directions, and students echo them step-by-step every time we write a letter. I mean, *every time* we write a letter. For example, my oral directions for the letter *e* are: "out from the middle and all around." We say it repeatedly until they say it when they are writing independently.

Big 3 Song—This isn't on display, but we sing it with hand motions at the beginning of each writing lesson. I get the biggest thrill when I see students singing it to themselves to check for the Big 3 in their writing (capitals to start, spaces in between, end mark to stop). The *Big 3 Song* can be found on page 66.

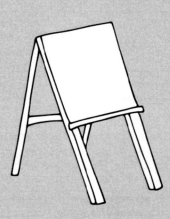

Implementing Writing Instruction *(cont.)*

Independent Writing

Independent writing occurs in two main ways: writing centers and journal writing.

Writing Centers

Once an activity has been taught and practiced several times as a whole group, it can be assigned as a center and used for independent practice. Centers are designed so students can be successful in writing independently because they are familiar with the structure of the activity; however, the content is replaced. Of course, there may be some students who need additional support in the center. I have provided some of the supports I use at each center in the descriptions. Each student's needs are slightly different, so if you see a child struggling to complete an activity independently at a center, note what the difficulty is, and then try to figure out a support to help them be successful.

Journal Writing

I usually begin journal writing around the 11th or 12th week of school. This gives me time at the beginning of the school year to acclimate students to school, introduce them to the idea that they are writers, and to teach a variety of spelling strategies so they can successfully write independently. I spend a lot of time teaching my students strategies for writing and how to use the tools posted in the room (e.g., *Sentence Maker*, page 91, and sentence starters posted on the word wall, page 74). Once students have the confidence to realize they can write, one of the main issues with getting them to write is the ability to generate topics for writing. A lesson on generating topics is provided (pages 99–102) and is important for helping students write independently. I have also had a lot of success helping students with topics by providing each student a CVC picture card (page 40) and having them use that picture as the topic. For all these methods of journal writing, it is crucial that modeling occurs for students so they know exactly what to do when it is time for them to write independently. A lesson to introduce journal writing is provided on pages 119–121.

Writing Folders—Provide students with two-prong folders to serve as a place to store tools for writing and their independent writing. The front pocket holds the *Author Idea List* (page 102) and current writing projects. The back pocket is for storing completed works. The prongs can have sheet protectors with a *Sentence Maker*, a personal word wall, sentence starters, and the *Big 3 Weekly Rubric* (see Digital Resources).

Word Wall, Sound Chart, and Vowel Charts—The word wall, sound chart, and vowel charts are especially important tools. These charts are useful every time students write, and it is important that they are constantly available for you to reference as you instruct and for students as they write. Be sure to dedicate some space in your classroom where these charts will be housed all year. See the Digital Resources for color copies of the sound chart and vowel charts.

Anchor Charts

Anchor charts are a critical part of each classroom, created to "anchor" knowledge. Students at the emergent level can refer to these charts to foster independence. Here are a few guidelines for making anchor charts:

 Students must help create the anchor chart. In an ideal setting, students will interactively write the words while placing the pictures on or adding illustrations to the chart.

 Text on anchor charts should be written in bold colors with block lettering. Charts should be simple, while still providing the needed information.

 Anchor charts should be placed so they can be seen throughout the room, at first, and can be moved to a center or specific area later. Charts can plaster every part of the room and can be removed when students stop using them.

 If the walls are white, and the chart paper is white, creating a border with marker can set the chart apart from the wall.

Implementing Writing Instruction *(cont.)*

Anchor Charts *(cont.)*

 Establish routines and demonstrate to students how to use an anchor chart. Remind them to use it if they don't.

It is assumed that once an anchor chart is created, it is posted in the room and available for students to reference.

Here are some don'ts for anchor charts:

 Don't premake an anchor chart. If you want students to be invested in it and use it, they need to be part of the process of making it. This creates ownership.

 Likewise, anchor charts should not be made, laminated, and kept year after year. Although charts are often the same from year to year, they can be personalized for each group of students. For example, when making a digraph anchor chart, I added *Shelby* and *Charlie*, because they were in our class. It meant more to that class. It gave them a connection.

The Word Wall

The word wall is the most important anchor chart in the early learning classroom. The word wall should occupy a prominent space in the room and must be physically and visually accessible to all students, whether they are at their desks, in centers, or on the carpet.

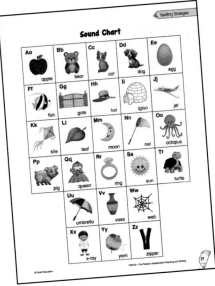

Creating the Word Wall

If wall space is unavailable, space on doors, cabinets, and boards will work as long as the word wall is clearly defined and accessible. Word wall headers are made by creating a card for each letter of the alphabet. Post these on the wall, and post enlarged pictures and words from the *Sound Chart* (page 17) next to the letters. Young learners benefit from seeing the same pictures and words on the word wall, the sound chart, and other resources in the room. Create a section labeled *Phrases* to provide a space for linking word-wall words together. Using a large, primary font on cards that are not laminated will ensure that all students can see the words.

Ideally, a word wall is interactive, enabling students to remove, use, and replace each word as needed. To facilitate this, use a magnetic board and attach magnets to the word cards. Another option is to add library pockets, labeled with letters along the bottom of the word wall. As new words are introduced and added to the word wall, duplicates can be placed in the pockets, making them accessible to young learners. If an interactive word wall isn't an option, create a space below the word wall where students can bring their writing and reference the words.

Word-Wall Words

For early learners, word-wall words should be high-frequency words that students are exposed to repeatedly during reading, such as those in beginning level readers. Your school district may provide lists of words required for your students. Dolch or Fry word lists are also good resources for high-frequency words. Word-wall words for early learners should be those that do not follow phonetic rules and those that students use often during writing but consistently misspell.

Do not include names, proper nouns, or content-specific words on the word wall. Instead, create a separate name chart with pictures of students, and use other interactive boards or anchor charts for content vocabulary.

Implementing Writing Instruction *(cont.)*

Word-Wall Guidelines

1. Begin the school year with *only* the alphabet headers on the word wall.

2. As new words are introduced and practiced with students, add them to the word wall.

3. Review all the words daily to develop recognition and understanding for students.

4. Teach students how to use the word wall for reading, writing, spelling, decoding, and making connections with known words. Establish routines for taking and returning words to the wall.

5. As the year progresses, hold students accountable for spelling words on the word wall correctly. During shared writing, consistently use the word wall, modeling how to find words and what to do if a word is not on the wall (see *How to Spell a Word* anchor chart on page 49). The Phrases section of the word wall can be used for sentence starters for reading and writing practice.

Cathy's Connections

Generally, adding two words per week to the word wall is appropriate for kindergartners. During the week, introduce and practice new words, and then move them to the word wall on Fridays. As you add words to the word wall, be sure to discuss, compare, and use them in context so students are empowered to own, interact with, and reference the wall.

Have fun with the words. Reviewing the words on the wall in ways that include multiple modalities is energizing, and it provides opportunities for all students to learn and use the words. For example, have students march as they say, spell, and say a word, or clap on the vowels as they spell a word aloud.

Sequence for Writing Instruction

Week(s)			Writing Lesson	Page
Introduce	Ongoing Whole Group	Center		
1	3–36	3	Sound Chart	15
1			Echo Writing for Color Words	18
2	3–9		Counting Words and Fold and Whisper	52
2	3–9		Echo Writing	18
2	3–18	18–36	Sentence Maker	89
3	4–9		4 to Score! Illustrations	54
3	4–9	7–18	Configuration Box Writing	23
3	4–9		The Big 3	60
3	4–9		Stretch-a-Word	22
9	10–18	19–36	Squiggle Writing	103
10	11–18	15–27	Stoplight Writing	37
10	11–18	15–27	Build-a-Sentence	67
10	11–18	19–36	Four-Square Target Writing	75
10	11–18		Predictable Sentences	72
10	10–12	13–36	Independent Journals	119
19	20–27		Think of a Word You Already Know	42
19	20–27		Use Resources to Find Words	45
19	20–27		How to Spell a Word	49
19	20–27	28–36	First, Then, Last	81
19	20–27		What to Write About	99
28	29–36		Opinion Writing	108
28	29–36	30–36	Narrative Writing	115

Sound Chart

Overview

A sound chart provides oral, written, and picture clues students can access when reading and writing independently. It is also used by the teacher during lessons.

Materials

- *Sound Chart* (page 17; enlarge to 200% or see Digital Resources for a color version)
- student copies of *Sound Chart* (page 17)

Procedure

1. Gather students around the *Sound Chart*, and describe its purpose. Say, "I'm excited to share our sound chart with you. This is one of the most important charts in our room. It will help us learn our letters and sounds and read, spell, and write clearly."

2. Tell students to echo as you describe how to use the chart. Say, "First, we will learn how to chant the chart. I'll say the letter, the sound, and then the word. I'm also going to use my hands for a rhythm. I will slap my legs, clap my hands, and snap my fingers, like this." Demonstrate: *a* (slap legs), /*a*/ (clap hands), *apple* (snap fingers). Have students echo the procedure. Reassure students who may not know how to snap. Say, "Don't worry if you can't snap. We can *fake it 'til we make it.*"

3. Lead the chant and hand motions for all the letters. Keep the chant going at a peppy pace. Slow down when you come to the letter *x*. *X* is a double sound, combining /*k*/ and /*s*/. Slowing down ensures that students will hear both sounds and better approximate saying them together. Pronounce each sound clearly and precisely. Ensure students are not adding a short *u* to the end of the letters, such as *d*, *g*, and *p* (i.e., *duh, guh, puh*).

4. Enlarge the *Sound Chart*, and keep it displayed in the room. Place student copies of the *Sound Chart* in homework folders so parents know the words and pictures their children are connecting to letters and sounds. In the classroom, include the chart in writing folders, independent reading boxes, and learning centers. Encourage students to reference the chart during whole-class and independent activities.

Cathy's Connections

I begin using the sound chart on the first day of school. Establishing a solid connection between a letter, sound, and picture helps solidify the names and sounds of the letters. We start each day with the sound chart and chant. At the beginning of the year, students echo my chant, one letter at a time. By November, we chorally chant the sound chart together. Fridays are backward days! We chant starting at *Z* and ending at *A*. In December, we choose a column on the chart and chant the letters going down the column. For consistency, I use the same sound chart for lessons, practice, word wall headers, and a letter/sound practice book.

Sound Chart (cont.)

Sound Chart Center

Students will match letters to the *Sound Chart* letters, pictures, and words.

Materials

- magnetic letters or letter tiles
- *Sound Chart* (page 17)

Activities

Encourage practice with the *Sound Chart* by teaching students how to use it as a center activity.

- Have students match magnetic letters or letter tiles to the corresponding letters on the *Sound Chart*.

- As students become proficient, have them use the magnetic letters or letter tiles to spell the words on the *Sound Chart*.

- Cut up the *Sound Chart*, and have students sort the pictures and words by beginning, middle, and ending sounds; number of syllables; and other categories.

   © Shell Education

Sound Chart

Aa apple	**Bb** bear	**Cc** cat	**Dd** dog	**Ee** egg
Ff fish	**Gg** gate	**Hh** hat	**Ii** igloo	**Jj** jet
Kk kite	**Ll** leaf	**Mm** moon	**Nn** net	**Oo** octopus
Pp pig	**Qq** queen	**Rr** ring	**Ss** sun	**Tt** turtle
	Uu umbrella	**Vv** vase	**Ww** web	
	Xx x-ray	**Yy** yarn	**Zz** zipper	

Echo Writing

Overview

Echo Writing is a form of shared writing during which the teacher models and describes the strokes for each letter. Students immediately mimic the teacher. It can be used with an individual student, a small group, or the whole class.

Materials

- *Penmanship Oral Directions* (pages 20–21)
- chart paper
- small whiteboard

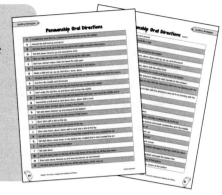

Procedure

1. Seat students on the carpet. Select a student volunteer to write on the chart paper.

2. Say, "Today, we are going to write the sentence *Here is a leaf.* As we write the words, you are going to echo *how* to make the letters I am writing." Lead students in Counting Words (pages 52–53).

3. Say, "Let's write the first word in the sentence. What is the first word?" (*Here*) Next say, "We are all going to write the letters in the word *Here* together. I'll write it on the board while you write it with your fingers and a helper will write it on the chart."

4. Tell the class to echo what you say and have everyone write the first letter in the air. Then, repeat the echoing while you write the letter on the small whiteboard and the students write it on their legs. Repeat the echoing again as the student helper writes on the chart paper and the rest of the students write on the carpet. Repeat these steps for each letter. Use *Penmanship Oral Directions* to describe the strokes.

   - Say, "Let's make an *H*. Tall stick down, *tall stick down*; tall stick down, *tall stick down*; across in the middle, *across in the middle.*"

   - "Let's make an *e*. Out from the middle and all around, *out from the middle and all around.*"

   - "Next, let's make an *r*. Short stick down, bounce up and a little around, *short stick down, bounce up and a little around.*"

   - "Finally, we need to make a letter that we don't hear. When we stretch the word *here*, we hear the *h, e*, and *r*, but this word has a long vowel sound. This time, we have a silent *e* at the end of the word. So, let's write an *e* at the end of our word. Out from the middle and all around, *out from the middle and all around.*"

Before a shared writing experience, draw faint pencil lines on chart paper or board for students to use as a guide. Show students how their letters should sit on the line or hang down. Guide them during Echo Writing with your finger for strokes that start in the middle of a letter or those that need to be crossed in the middle or at the top, such as a lowercase *t* or capital *I*. Use the pointer/spacer to demonstrate appropriate spacing between words.

Echo Writing (cont.)

Procedure (cont.)

5. After writing the entire word, read the word and use Counting Words and Fold and Whisper (pages 52–53) to help students keep track of the words in the sentence.

6. Continue, writing each word using Echo Writing, making sure that students echo and "write" stroke by stroke. Use Counting Words and Fold and Whisper after writing each word.

7. At the end of the lesson say, "I love the way you are using your words to help you make letters as we are writing."

Cathy's Connections

Create a "freezer moment" when you are writing with students and encounter a word with a vowel pattern or other pattern that hasn't yet been taught. Give students a brief explanation, and tell them they will learn about it later. This allows you to "put it in the freezer" and "take it out" when students are academically ready.

For example, for the word *leaf*, you would use Stretch-a-Word (page 22) to discover the /l/, /ē/, and /f/ sounds with the class. After writing the *l* and *e*, you could then say, "Usually when we hear a long vowel sound, there are two vowels. In this word, we heard a long *e* sound, so we wrote an *e*, but there is also an *a* that we don't hear. I'll write the *a*, and then we need to stretch the word again to write the ending sound." This provides a quick explanation about why there are two vowels, without a lengthy lesson.

Penmanship Oral Directions

A	Crooked line from the top; crooked line from the top; across the middle
a	Around the ball and up and down
B	Tall stick down; back up to the top; around to the middle; around to the bottom
b	Tall stick down; bounce up and around the ball
C	Start up high; almost make a big ball, but leave the side open
c	Start low; almost make a ball, but leave the side open
D	Tall stick down; back up to the top and curve around to the bottom
d	Around the ball and up, up, up, and down, down, down
E	Tall stick down; back up to the top; out from the top; out from the middle; out from the bottom
e	Out from the middle and all around
F	Tall stick down; back up to the top; out from the top; out from the middle
f	Start under the top line with an arch; up and down and across the middle
G	Start up high; almost make a big ball and leave the side open and up to the middle and in
g	Around the ball and up and down, down, down with a hook
H	Tall stick down; tall stick down; across in the middle
h	Tall stick down; bounce up and around to the bottom
I	Tall stick down; across at the top; across at the bottom
i	Short stick down with a dot on the top
J	Tall stick down with a hook and across at the top
j	Short stick down, down, down with a hook and a dot at the top
K	Tall stick down; move away on the top line; slant line in and crooked line out
k	Tall stick down; move away on the dotted line; crooked line in and crooked line out
L	Tall stick down; out from the bottom
l	Tall stick down
M	Tall stick down; back to the top; all the way down; all the way up; all the way down
m	Short stick down; bounce up and around; bounce up and around
N	Tall stick down; back up to the top; all the way down; all the way up

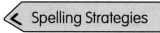

Penmanship Oral Directions *(cont.)*

n	Short stick down; bounce up and around
O	Around the ball from the top
o	Around the ball from the middle
P	Tall stick down; back up to the top; around to the middle
p	Start in the middle; short stick down, down, down and up, up, up, and all around
Q	Start at the top; make a big circle and around; crooked line cross at the bottom
q	Make a ball and up and down, down, down with the other hook
R	Tall stick down; back up to the top; around to the middle and back out to the bottom
r	Short stick down; bounce up and a little around (I make my voice squeak on this phrase.)
S	To the left, to the right, to the left (I swing my hips with the directions and call it my *Dancing with the Stars* letter.)
s	To the left, to the right, to the left (I swing my hips with the directions and call it my *Dancing with the Stars* letter.)
T	Tall stick down; across at the top
t	Tall stick down; across in the middle
U	Tall stick down and around and up
u	Like a smile; down and up and straight back down
V	Start at the top; big crooked line down to the bottom and big crooked line up to the top
v	Start in the middle; small crooked line down to the bottom and small crooked line up to the middle
W	Start at the top; four crooked lines; down, up, down, up
w	Start in the middle; four crooked lines; down, up, down, up
X	Big crooked line to the bottom; big crooked line back across
x	Small crooked line to the bottom; small crooked line back across
Y	Start at the top; small crooked line to the middle; jump out at the top; small crooked line down to the middle; small line down from the middle
y	Small crooked line to the bottom; long crooked line coming back and past the bottom line
Z	Start at the top; across the top, crooked to the bottom; across at the bottom
z	Start at the middle; across the middle, crooked to the bottom; across at the bottom

Stretch-a-Word

Overview

Teaching students Stretch-a-Word lays the groundwork for independent writing and reading. Stretching words aids students' understanding of the relationships between letters and sounds.

Materials

- one large rubber band
- *Sound Chart* (page 17)
- small whiteboard
- Vowel Charts (see Digital Resources)

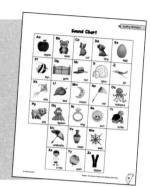

Procedure

1. Seat students on the floor so they can easily see your mouth. They should also be able to see the word wall, Sound Chart, and Vowel Charts displayed in the room.

2. Say, "Today, we are going to talk about stretching a word." Ask students what it means to stretch something. Show students the large rubber band and stretch it. Have them put a pretend rubber band in their hands and stretch it. You can even *sssttrrreeettccchhh* the word *stretch* as you stretch the rubber band. Have students pretend to chew a piece of bubble gum and stretch it and chew it some more. Giggle a little about doing this, reminding them that it might not be the best manners to chew gum this way.

3. Say, "Stretching words is the same as stretching a rubber band or bubble gum. We stretch out the words and think about the sounds in them." Tell students that today they will write the word *cab*—like a taxi cab. Say, "Let's stretch *cab*. Put the word in your mouth, and chew on it for a second." As you pretend to chew, say the word *cab* several times. Then, begin stretching it into three parts by saying "/*cccc*/-/*aaaa*/-/*bbbb*/." Invite students to stretch the word with you.

4. Model using the *Sound Chart* to figure out the corresponding letters for the word. Say, "Stretch it again, and stop after the first sound, /*cccc*/. I think that sounds like the /*c*/ in *cat*. Does it sound the same to you? Which letter makes the /*c*/ sound?" Affirm the correct answers, and have a student volunteer go to the sound chart and point to the *c*.

5. Continue by saying, "We are going to write a *c*." Use Echo Writing (pages 18–19) to demonstrate how to make the *c* on a small whiteboard. Have students echo the directions while they use their index fingers to write on the carpet. Have a student helper write the *c* on the board.

6. Repeat the stretching and writing routine for the rest of the word *cab*. When listening for the vowel, direct students to use the Vowel Charts to identify the correct letter. Practice stretching other suggested CVC words during this lesson or on subsequent days.

7. End the lesson with a review by saying, "Let's talk about what we do when we get to a word we don't know how to spell. The strategy we talked about today was Stretch-a-Word. What can we think of to help us remember how to stretch a word?" (Possible answers include a rubber band and bubble gum.) "We're going to practice this strategy a lot this year, and you are going to be great at writing new words."

Cathy's Connections

Adding a yellow dot to the vowels on the sound chart or adding Vowel Cards to your word wall can help with those "tricky" vowels that make spellers "slow down."

Configuration Box Writing—Day 1

Overview

This lesson is taught to students over five consecutive days. Configuration boxes provide size and shape models for early handwriting practice. Students practice writing letters with proper size formation and placement on a line.

Materials

- chart paper
- *Letters That I Write* (page 24)
- *Penmanship Oral Directions* (pages 20–21)

Preparation

Prepare a Letter Configuration anchor chart by drawing three columns on a sheet of chart paper. At the top of each column, draw writing lines—top line, mid-line, and bottom line. Write lowercase *h* in the left column, lowercase *u* in the middle column, and lowercase *g* in the right column. Add a red line with arrows indicating the space each letter takes.

Procedure

1. Seat students around the chart. Say, "We have been writing a lot of words, and I have been telling you how to make the letters. Today, we are going to learn a song about the letters! It will help you write your letters by yourselves."

2. Direct students' attention to the anchor chart. Tell them that this chart shows three kinds of letters they can make. These include:

   - **tall letters** (point to the *h*)—"This *h* starts at the top line and goes to the bottom line." (Trace the *h* from the top line to the bottom line.)

   - **small letters** (point to the *u*)—"Notice that this letter *u* starts at the dotted line and goes to the bottom line." (Trace the *u* from the dotted line to the bottom line.)

   - **hang-down letters** (point to the *g*)—"This *g* starts at the dotted line and swings below the bottom line." (Trace the *g* from the dotted line to below the bottom line.)

3. Say, "I am going to sing a song about the three kinds of letters. It is called 'Letters That I Write.'" Ask students to listen for the three kinds of letters listed on the anchor chart. Sing the song to the tune of "London Bridge Is Falling Down."

4. Say, "Did you hear the three ways to make letters in the song? Now that we know we can make letters three ways, let's add to our chart to show more letters that are tall letters, small letters, or hang-down letters."

5. Write letters on the board, and ask students to help you identify the kinds of letters they are. Use Echo Writing (pages 18–19), and have students write the letters in the air as you write them on the anchor chart. After each letter, review its placement on the lines, and have students repeat the correct term—tall, small, or hang down. Model at least two letters in each column.

6. Close by asking, "Why do you think it's important to know about letters and how they look on paper?" Affirm students by saying, "Yes, because it makes what we write easy to read. It is very important that other people can read what we write."

7. Save the Letter Configuration anchor chart for Day 2.

Letters That I Write

(sung to the tune of "London Bridge Is Falling Down")

Letters I write are made 3 ways,
    Made 3 ways; made 3 ways. (*Hold 3 fingers up and bounce on the words "made 3 ways".*)

Letters I write are made 3 ways,
    Helps me write clearly.

Some of the letters are tall-tall-tall,
    tall-tall-tall, tall-tall-tall. (*Stand on tiptoes, and stretch hands to the ceiling.*)

They start at the top and go straight down,
    Taller than them all. (*Point to the ceiling, and pull down the line.*)

Some of the letters are small-small-small,
    small-small-small, small-small-small, (*Stand up straight and hold your arms in front of you as if you are holding a watermelon.*)

They start at the dots and go to the line,
    Smaller than them all. (*Use your index finger to point out straight in front of you. Make a short motion straight down about 12 inches.*)

Some of the letters they hang on down,
    hang on down, hang on down, (*Bend over. Swing your right arm down like a monkey tail, back and forth.*)

They start at the dots and hang on down,
    Swing below the ground. (*Use your index finger to point out straight in front of you. Make a motion straight down, and then curve it at the end.*)

Configuration Box Writing—Day 2

Materials

- Letter Configuration anchor chart (from Day 1)
- one set of *Lowercase Alphabet Cards* (pages 26–28); cut apart
- tape or magnets

Procedure

1. Seat students around the Letter Configuration anchor chart. Say, "Yesterday, I sang the 'Letters That I Write' song to help you learn the three kinds of letters. We also wrote some letters on our chart. Let's sing the song again. Sing along with me today." Sing the "Letters That I Write" song.

2. Review the three kinds of letters by calling on three students to identify each kind of letter on the chart. Ask questions to help students notice the formation of the letters that are already on the chart. For example, "Where does the letter start?" "Where does the letter end?" "Does the letter hang down?"

3. Distribute one letter card to each student. Ask students to talk with partners to determine in which columns their letters belong.

4. Have students place their letters in the correct columns on the chart. Affix the letter cards with tape or magnets. Encourage students to use the words *tall, small,* or *hang down* to describe their letters.

5. After all the letters are placed on the chart, say, "I am so impressed with the chart we made today. This chart will help us when we write."

6. Save the Letter Configuration anchor chart for Day 3.

Lowercase Alphabet Cards

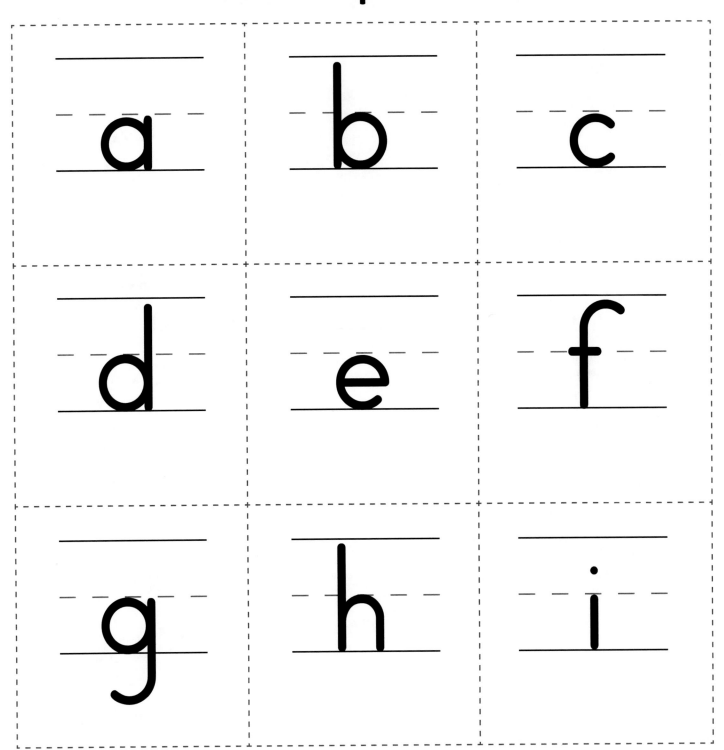

j k l

m n o

p q r

Lowercase Alphabet Cards *(cont.)*

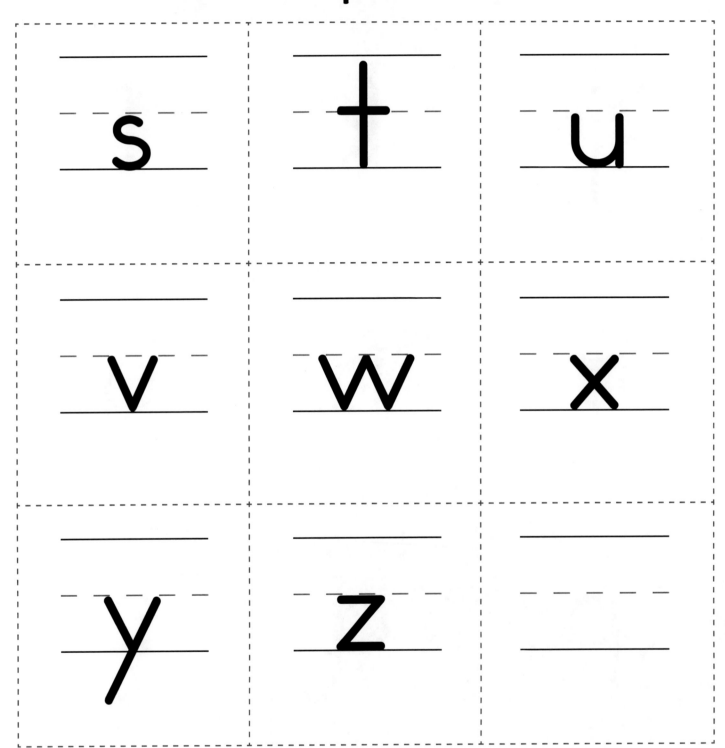

124548—The Road to Independent Reading and Writing © Shell Education

Configuration Box Writing—Day 3

Materials

- Letter Configuration anchor chart (from Days 1 and 2)
- *Three Kinds of Letters Pictures* (page 30; see Digital Resources for a color version)

Procedure

1. Seat students around the Letter Configuration anchor chart. Say, "Let's sing the 'Letters That I Write' song to help us remember the three ways to make letters." Sing the song.

2. Review the anchor chart showing the three ways to make letters. Ask questions, such as "Where does the letter start?" "Where does the letter end?" "Does the letter hang down?" Encourage students to use the words *tall*, *small*, or *hang down* when describing the letters.

3. Show students the *Three Kinds of Letters Pictures*. Say, "Today, we are going to play a game with these letters. I will say the name of a letter, and you will use your bodies to show if it is a tall letter, small letter, or hang-down letter." Demonstrate each type of letter described, and have students practice.

   - **tall letter**—stand on tiptoes and stretch to reach the ceiling so you look tall like a giraffe
   - **small letter**—stand up straight and pretend to hold a watermelon in front of you
   - **hang-down letter**—bend over and swing your hand like a monkey's tail

4. Name letters, and have students position their bodies like a giraffe, panda bear, or monkey. Coach students through the first few letters. Then, allow students to play without coaching.

5. After students have practiced several letters, say, "Wow, that was fun practicing the letters. I think this will really help me remember what type of letter I'm trying to write and how to write it correctly."

Three Kinds of Letters Pictures

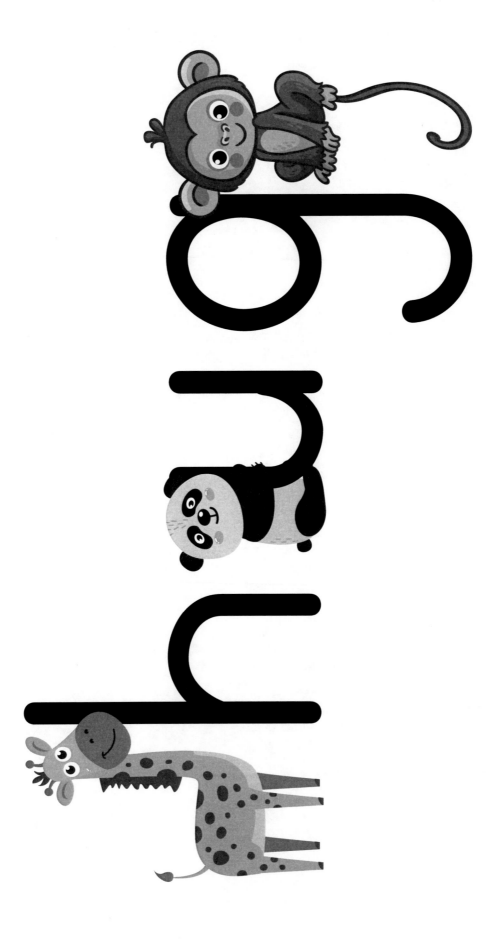

Configuration Box Writing—Day 4

Materials

* *Configuration Box Words* (page 32); replicate on a sheet of chart paper
* student copies of *Configuration Box Words* (page 32)

Procedure

1. Seat students around the prepared Configuration Box Words chart. Say, "Let's write some words using different letter sizes. We are going to use these boxes. (Point to the chart.) Some of the boxes are tall for tall letters, some are small for small letters, and some hang down for our hang-down letters."

2. Write the word *big* on the board. Direct students' attention to the first set of boxes on the chart. Say, "Let's look at the letters in the word *big*. I see a tall box, a small box, and a hang-down box. If I look at the word *big*, *b* is a tall letter, *i* is a small letter, and *g* is a hang-down letter."

3. Say, "Stand up, and let's spell *big* with our bodies." Lead students in using their bodies to show the tall letter, small letter, and hang-down letter in the word *big*. Then say, "Now, have a seat and we'll write the letters in the boxes, making sure the *b* is tall, the *i* is small, and the *g* hangs down."

4. Write each letter on the chart. Say, "Let's spell the word *big* out loud while you point to the letters." Once students have pointed to the letters and spelled the word, say, "Let's look at the boxes and write the letters correctly. What is the first letter? (*b*) What kind of letter is *b*? (*tall*) Watch while I write the tall *b* in the tall box." Show students how to make the *b* fill the box on the Configuration Box Words chart.

5. Follow the routine with the letters *i* and *g*. Continually ask students questions to involve them in the process. "What letter comes next?" "What type of letter is it?" "Can you use your body to show if it is a tall letter, small letter, or hang-down letter?"

6. Repeat the process for the words *good* and *happy*. Involve students by asking for volunteers to help write the letters on the chart. Make sure these letters fill the boxes correctly.

7. When the Configuration Box Words chart is complete, have students go to their seats. Distribute copies of *Configuration Box Words* to students. Point to the word *big* on the chart, and say, "Now it's time for you to practice writing some words using our three kinds of letters. Make sure to fill up the boxes with each letter, just like the ones on this chart."

8. Start by working with the whole group to complete the first word. Allow students who are ready to move ahead to finish the activity independently. Monitor students as they work, reminding them as needed about the shapes of the letters and how they fit in the boxes.

9. When students have finished, say, "This was a fun writing lesson today, wasn't it? We made the words with our bodies and our pencils! I am excited to see you make your letters correctly."

Configuration Box Words

Directions: Write the words.

big=

good=

happy=

Configuration Box Writing—Day 5

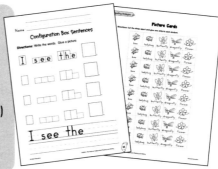

Materials

- *Configuration Box Sentences* (page 35); replicate on chart paper for display, and draw an apple on the line at the end of the first sentence
- student copies of *Configuration Box Sentences* (page 35)
- one strip per student of *Picture Cards* (page 36); cut apart so each student has a row of five pictures

Procedure

1. Seat students around the prepared Configuration Box Sentences chart. Say, "We have been practicing writing words using boxes to help us make our letters correctly. Today, we are going to do a little more. We are going to write sentences using the boxes. Let's read this sentence together. *I see the* (*apple*)."

2. Next, say, "Let's make the words with our bodies. Stand up and show me how to make the letter *I*. Are you standing on your tiptoes with your arms in the air? Great job. Watch as I write the letter *I* in its box." As you write *I*, remind students that you are filling up the box from top to bottom. Remind students that the *I* is capital because it is the first letter/word in the sentence.

3. Say, "Now, let's write the word *see*. All three of these letters are short letters. Let's pretend to hold a ball and spell the word." Say each letter as you pretend to hold a ball. Write *see* in the boxes on the chart, reminding students to completely fill the short boxes with the letters.

4. Continue demonstrating how to write each word, letter by letter. As you write, comment on how to fill the configuration boxes.

5. Have students go to their seats. Distribute copies of *Configuration Box Sentences* and strips of five picture cards to students.

6. Lead students step-by-step through completing the first sentence. Tell them to write the letters, one box at a time, from left to right.

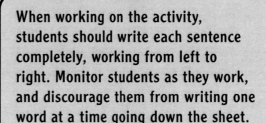

> When working on the activity, students should write each sentence completely, working from left to right. Monitor students as they work, and discourage them from writing one word at a time going down the sheet.

7. After students write the sentence starter, have them choose a picture to finish the sentence, cut it out, and glue it on the line. Have students read their sentences to a desk partner.

8. Have students finish the activity independently. Point out that at the bottom of the sheet, there are lines for students to write sentences without using the boxes and picture cards. Encourage each student to choose a picture card and stretch the word to spell it or to look at the sound chart or other anchor charts in the room to find the correct spelling.

9. Circulate around the room, encouraging students to use correct letter formation. As students finish the activity, have them read their sentences to their desk partners or adults in the room.

10. Close by saying, "This was a fun writing lesson today, wasn't it? We made the words with our bodies and our pencils! I am so excited to see you make your letters correctly."

Configuration Box Writing—Day 5 *(cont.)*

Cathy's Connections

Typically, the words selected for configuration box activities are words students will write frequently. Teachers can differentiate for reading and writing levels. Some students can glue and read the pictures, while other students can write words to complete the sentences using words from the sound chart or other resources in the classroom.

Configuration Box Writing Center

Students will write words and sentences using configuration boxes to make tall, small, or hang-down letters.

Materials

- *Configuration Box Sentences* (page 35; see Digital Resources for additional practice pages)
- *Picture Cards* (page 36; see Digital Resources for additional picture cards)

Activities

Encourage independent practice with writing sentences in configuration boxes with this center.

- Provide students with additional practice using new sentences. See Digital Resources for additional student practice pages with a variety of sentences.

- Encourage students to write their own words in the blanks by phonetically sounding out the words.

- As students become more proficient, transition them to writing their own sentences at this center rather than using the configuration boxes.

- Support students having difficulty doing this activity independently by writing the first sentence they would write using a highlighter. Students can trace the highlighter as their first attempt at writing each letter.

Name _____

Configuration Box Sentences

Directions: Write the words. Glue a picture.

I see the ☐ .

☐ ☐ ☐ ☐ .

☐ ☐ ☐ ☐ .

☐ ☐ ☐ ☐ .

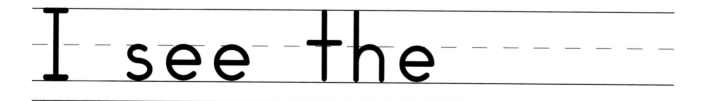

I see the

Picture Cards

Directions: Cut the strips apart horizontally and give one strip to each student.

bee	ladybug	butterfly	dragonfly	flower
bee	ladybug	butterfly	dragonfly	flower
bee	ladybug	butterfly	dragonfly	flower
bee	ladybug	butterfly	dragonfly	flower
bee	ladybug	butterfly	dragonfly	flower
bee	ladybug	butterfly	dragonfly	flower
bee	ladybug	butterfly	dragonfly	flower
bee	ladybug	butterfly	dragonfly	flower

Stoplight Writing

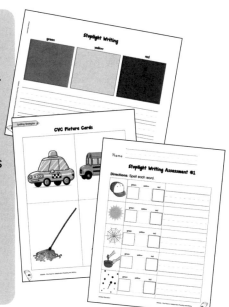

Overview

Students will use graphic organizers to write CVC words. The organizer provides a resource for students to independently spell and write new words.

Materials

- student copies of *Stoplight Writing* (page 39; see Digital Resources for a color version, or use a green, yellow, and red crayon to outline the boxes on students' papers)
- dry erase pockets or heavy duty sheet protectors and markers; one per student
- *CVC Picture Cards* (page 40)
- student copies of *Stoplight Writing Assessment #1* (page 41; see Digital Resources for additional color versions)

Procedure

1. Distribute copies of *Stoplight Writing* and dry erase markers and pockets to students. Tell students to slip the papers into the pockets. Display an example of the *Stoplight Writing* paper so students can see it.

2. Say, "Today, we are going to practice writing words. A word is like a story. They both have a beginning, a middle, and an end. We are going to practice writing the beginning, middle, and end of a word."

3. Continue by saying, "There are three boxes on your paper. One is green, one is yellow, and one is red. What can you think of that has these three colors? What do the colors mean?" (A stoplight. The colors mean *go*, *slow*, and *stop*.) "Why do you think the boxes are three colors?" Lead student responses to conclude that green will be the beginning, yellow will be the middle, and red will be the end of a word.

4. Say, "Let's use the Stretch-a-Word (page 22) strategy for a word. Listen carefully to all its parts." Hold up the *cab* picture card. Say, "Look at this picture. What is it? Right, it's a cab. Let's stretch that word just like you can stretch a rubber band or bubble gum: /ccccc/ /aaaa/ /bbbb/."

5. Say, "What sound do you hear at the beginning of the word *cab*? Let's stretch it and stop, /cccc/. Look at the sound chart. Does the /c/ sound like *cat* or sound like *moon*?" After students respond, say, "I hear /c/ like *cat*. Listen, /c/ *cat* and /c/ *cab*. Does it sound the same to you? Which letter makes the /c/ sound?" Affirm the correct answers, and have a student volunteer point to the *c* on the *Sound Chart*.

Stoplight Writing *(cont.)*

Procedure *(cont.)*

6. Guide students to write the letter for the first sound by pointing to the example on *Stoplight Writing* and saying, "Let's write a *c* in the first box. That's the green box on the stoplight. Green means go." Model how to make the *c* using Echo Writing (pages 18–19). Ask students to make a *c* in the air and on the carpet with their index fingers. Then, have students write the *c* on their papers.

7. Continue this process for the middle sound. Say, "On a stoplight, yellow usually means to slow down or be careful. The letter in the middle of this word is a vowel. Vowels are tricky, so we have to slow down and be careful." Does the middle letter sound like /a/ apple or /e/ egg? Write an *a* in the yellow box on *Stoplight Writing* using Echo Writing. Then, have students write the *a* on their papers.

8. Finally, ask students what red stands for on a stoplight, and say, "We stop at the red light or at the end of a word. We need to stretch the word all the way to the end." Use the *Sound Chart* to make connections to the ending letter. Then, use Echo Writing to write *b* on the example, and have students write it on their papers.

9. Finish the lesson by saying, "We did it! We wrote all the sounds in the word *cab*. Let's run our fingers under each letter as we say it."

Additional CVC picture cards are available in the Digital Resources.

Next Steps

Practice the Stoplight Writing routine each day with the class using different CVC words. As students are ready, challenge them to write the letters without prompts. Place the activity in a center for independent writing to help students gain confidence and automaticity when writing. Continue to discuss the sound/letter connections to the sound chart, and use Echo Writing for proper penmanship. Transition to students writing the letters on lines, but keep the stoplight boxes available as visual cues.

Cathy's Connections

Use the *Stoplight Writing Assessment #1* to monitor students' progress identifying the beginning, middle, and ending sounds. Students should write the words independently; however, you can help sound out the words. Say the individual sounds, then repeat the whole word. Do not make one sound and have them write one sound, then make another sound and have them write the next sound. Instead, make sure they say all the sounds in the word slightly separated, but then repeat the whole word.

Repeat this process for several weeks, using ongoing assessment data to determine who needs more intervention and who can move forward.

Stoplight Writing

green

yellow

red

CVC Picture Cards

Name _____

Stoplight Writing Assessment #1

Directions: Spell each word.

	green yellow red	
	□ □ □	_____
	green yellow red	
	□ □ □	_____
	green yellow red	
	□ □ □	_____
	green yellow red	
	□ □ □	_____
	green yellow red	
	□ □ □	_____

Think of a Word You Already Know

Overview

This strategy teaches students to use words they know how to spell to write words they don't know how to spell. Looking for connections between the phonemic and graphic representations of words can also be used as a reading strategy for decoding.

Materials

- *Think of a Word You Already Know* (page 44; replicate on chart paper, but omit the words in the second and third column and the thought bubbles so they can be filled in during the lesson; see Digital Resources for a color version)

Procedure

1. Say, "Today, we are going to learn a strategy for spelling a word we aren't sure how to spell. We are going to use a word we already know to help us spell a word we don't know."

2. Direct students' attention to the Think of a Word You Already Know chart, and say, "This chart will help us understand how to do this."

3. Say, "Let's look at the first row. In this row, I want to spell the word *bus*. I'm not sure how to spell the word *bus*, so I need to think of a word I know that is almost like the word *bus*. One place I can look is the word wall."

4. Say, "Let's look at the word wall to see if there is a word that sounds like the word *bus*." Say and stretch the word slowly. Repeat the word slowly, and walk toward the word wall. Stress the /b/ sound, and look directly at the *b* words on the word wall. Say, "I think I hear the same beginning and middle sounds in *bus* as I do in our word wall word *but*. Do you hear the same beginning and middle sounds?" Stretch the word slowly again with students.

Cathy's Connections

Stretch-a-Word (page 22) is an important skill for writing independently. In this lesson, students are asked to stretch words through the beginning, middle, and end. If a student writes a CVC word without the middle vowel, make a yellow dot where the vowel is missing to remind the student to add the vowel (Stoplight Writing, pages 37–41). Likewise, make a red dot if a CVC word is written without the ending letter.

Think of a Word You Already Know *(cont.)*

Procedure *(cont.)*

5. If the words on the word wall are removable, take the word card for *but* to the chart, and model how to refer to it while writing the word in the thinking bubble. If the words on the word wall are stapled, have a student volunteer find the word and "shout" the spelling to you while you write it and the class echoes it.

6. Have students say the words *bus* and *but*. Ask if they hear the *b* at the beginning of each word. Then, write the *b* in the New Word column. Repeat this for the middle sound.

7. Next, ask students if the ending of *bus* and the ending of *but* are the same. Stretch the word slowly to help students hear the difference. Ask students what sound is at the end of *bus*, and write the *s* on the chart. Compliment students on using a word from the word wall to spell a new word.

8. Show students the next row on the chart, and say, "Now, we will spell the word *fed*." Tap your finger on your temple to show you are thinking. Using the color chart, ask if there is a color word that sounds like the word *fed*. Hint that students could look for a rhyming word. When a student volunteers the word *red*, say, "Let's use *red* to spell the word *fed*."

9. Write the word *red* in the middle column, and draw a crayon around it to remind students to use color words or anchor charts in the room. Students can refer to the color chart and "shout" the spelling while you write the word.

10. Using the word wall, lead students in finding the beginning sound of *fed*. Talk students through the process of using the letter *f* to start the word and using the -*ed* from *red* to complete it. Compliment students on using a color word to spell a new word.

11. Finally, point to the picture of the *king* in the third row. Following a similar process, use the sound chart to help students make the connection between *king* and *ring*, and determine the beginning, middle, and ending sounds.

12. Summarize the activity by saying, "We can use resources in our room to help us spell new words. We can find words that we already know and use them to help us spell new words. Where did we find the words that helped us spell our new words?" (word wall, color chart, sound chart)

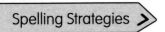

Think of a Word You Already Know

What you want to spell	What you know	New word
	but	bus
	Red	fed
	Rr ring	king

124548—The Road to Independent Reading and Writing

© Shell Education

Use Resources to Find Words—Day 1

Overview

This lesson is taught to students over three days. The teacher models how to use readily available resources, such as anchor charts and books, to help spell words. As students become familiar with this strategy, they will refer to these resources on their own during independent writing.

Materials

- chart paper

Procedure

1. Say, "Today, let's write about something we have read about before." Choose a topic that corresponds with a chart on display in the classroom and includes some longer words students do not know how to spell. For example, if you have an anchor chart with fall words, you could tell students you will be writing about a scarecrow.

2. Begin writing a sentence using the chosen word. When you come to the word, ask students where it can be found in the room. When a student identifies the chart the word is located on, ask him or her to walk to the chart and show the class the word.

3. Ask the student to "shout out" the spelling of the word as you write it in the sentence. Write another sentence or two using words displayed in the room. Each time, select students to show the class where they found the words and to "shout out" the spellings.

4. Say, "What a great idea (student's name) had to find the word _____ in our classroom. Try to use this strategy today when you are writing."

Use Resources to Find Words—Day 2

Materials
- chart paper

Procedure

1. Remind students that yesterday, they learned how to use resources in the room to find out how to spell words. Tell students that today, they will learn another strategy for how to spell words. Say, "I'm thinking of writing a story during journal time using some of the characters that we have been reading about in (book title)."

2. Tell students that you aren't sure how to write the characters' names correctly, but you are going to try. Say the names aloud as you write them. Use approximate spellings for the names (make the initial and final consonants correct).

3. With a puzzled look on your face, say, "These names don't look quite right to me. Does anyone know how to spell these names correctly or know where I can find them written correctly?"

4. When a student refers to the book, have them get the book and find one of the names. After finding the name, ask the student to show a friend and make sure it is the correct name.

5. Have the student "shout out" the spelling as you correct your initial spelling of the name. Follow this procedure for the other names.

6. Decide what the characters will do. If possible, select an activity based on students' current reading materials. For example, if a group of students is reading about a park, ask someone to use their book and find the word *park*.

7. Continue asking students to find key words in classroom books and to "shout out" the spellings as you write the sentences.

8. When you have completed the story, say, "I am so proud of the authors we are becoming. I think it was clever of (student's name) to suggest we use a book in our room to help find words for our own stories. Try to use this strategy today when you are writing."

Cathy's Connections

Students need to take pride in their writing skills. Teaching routines helps strengthen independence and is a powerful way to build this pride.

One of my struggling students was writing in his journal. He came running up to me and said, "Mrs. Collier! Can I go get my reading book (*The Big, Enormous Hamburger*) because I want my dog in my story to be enormous, not just big!" That's what we want!

Use Resources to Find Words—Day 3

Materials
- chart paper

. . . .

Procedure

1. Review the strategies of finding words in the room and in books that students learned the previous two days.

2. Say, "Let's talk about another strategy for when you don't know how to spell a word. What if I want to write about a bear, but I'm not sure how to spell *bear*? Instead of stopping my story or changing what I want to write about, I can find someone in our classroom to help me spell it or find it. Is there someone who can help me?"

3. Allow several students to suggest classroom resources where the word can be found (the sound chart, color chart, the word wall, classroom books, anchor charts). One student will inevitably say that he or she (or a classroom helper) could spell the word for a friend. When that happens, say, "We are all trying to grow as readers and writers. Should we tell our classmates *how* to spell words, or should we help them *find* the words so they can spell them on their own?"

4. Acknowledge several responses, and agree that helping *find* the words is a good strategy. Say, "I think the best way to learn something is to do it ourselves. We can ask for help, but doing it ourselves makes it more meaningful to us. If we were going to learn how to shoot a basketball and make it in the hoop, do we have to do it ourselves or can someone else do it for us?" (Acknowledge responses affirming that they should do it for themselves.) "That's right, we have to learn how to do it ourselves."

5. Continue by asking, "Can we ask for help about *how* to shoot a basket?" (Wait for affirmative responses.) "Having someone show us *how* to hold the ball correctly and *how* to move our arms is certainly okay, but if someone makes the shot for us, we aren't learning."

6. Say, "It's the same thing with writing or reading. We can help friends figure it out, but we shouldn't do it *for* them. Let's practice helping our friends *find* words."

7. Ask the class to help you spell some words that are displayed in the room (on the sound chart, color chart, word wall, or anchor charts). Ask for help, and have students practice the sentence frame *I'll help. You should look on the _____.* Model positively responding to this help by thanking students each time.

8. After role-playing this scenario with a few students, have all students practice with partners. To conclude the lesson, tell students that they should only use this strategy if they cannot find a word themselves.

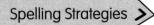

Use Resources to Find Words—Day 3 *(cont.)*

Cathy's Connections

Establishing a few simple protocols for this strategy will help ensure that it does not become overused by students, and that students asking for help become responsible for the spelling. Having students role-play helping one another will also create a classroom of helpers who want to aid their friends, not do it for them. When students ask adults in the room how to spell words, the adults should work with students to use Stretch-a-Word (page 22) or other strategies to determine the correct spellings.

How to Spell a Word—Day 1

Overview

This culminating activity takes place over two days and brings together all the strategies for determining the spelling of a word. Ideally, this anchor chart will be created with the class after introducing students to all the spelling strategies. This anchor chart will become an important resource for students during independent and shared writing.

Materials

- chart paper

Procedure

1. Say, "Sometimes, we want to write words we don't know how to spell. We have practiced what to do when this happens. Let's make a word web and write some ways to spell words we don't know."

2. Draw a large circle in the middle of the chart paper, and write *How to spell a word* in the circle. Read the phrase aloud, and ask, "What are some ways we can spell words?" Lead students to recall the lessons about Stretch-a-Word (page 22), Stoplight Writing (pages 37–41), and Use Resources to Find Words (pages 45–48).

3. As students offer ideas, ask them to come up and help you write one key word from each example on the anchor chart. For example, *stretch* and *think*.

4. When finished, say, "You have remembered many good strategies to use for finding how to spell a word. Tomorrow, we will decide when it is best to use them."

5. Save the How to Spell a Word anchor chart for Day 2.

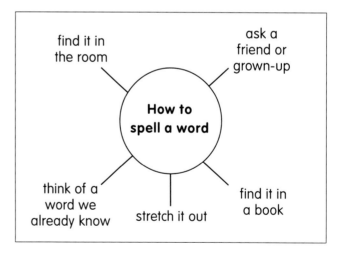

How to Spell a Word—Day 1 *(cont.)*

Cathy's Connections

Students should be able to write without fear of writing. Part of what students fear is spelling. As adults, we unintentionally teach students that they don't know how to spell something instead of teaching them *how* to spell. We say, "Let me spell that for you," "What does that say?," or "Let me show you how that should be spelled." We give the impression that students can't do it, so they should rely on us. Teaching spelling strategies reduces fear and encourages independence. As we teach the strategies, we should let students write, and their attempts at spelling words as they sound should be rewarded.

How to Spell a Word—Day 2

Materials

- How to Spell a Word anchor chart (from Day 1)
- chart paper
- five sentence strips
- tape or magnets

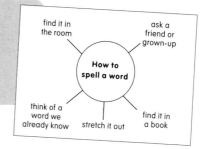

Procedure

1. Write the five strategies for ways to spell words (from Day 1) on sentence strips.

2. Say, "Yesterday, you remembered five ways to spell a word that you can use when writing." Review the anchor chart, and engage students in a discussion about which ideas they think are the most helpful or easiest to use.

3. Help students rank the strategies from most independent to most dependent. Tape the sentence strips to a sheet of chart paper in the order students determine. Ask students, "Which of these strategies can you do by yourself?" Acknowledge students' responses, and guide them to the conclusion that *ask a friend or grown-up* is not an independent strategy. Discuss with students reasons why this strategy should be a last resort.

4. At the end of the lesson, say, "I am really excited about this anchor chart! Having lots of ideas for spelling on your own helps you become independent learners and gets you ready to write what you want, when you want."

How to Spell an Unknown Word

1. Find it in the room.

2 Think of a word we already know. look = book

3. Stretch it out.

4. Find it in a book.

5. Ask a friend or grown-up.

Cathy's Connections

The option of *ask a friend or grown-up* may sound very appealing and helpful to kindergarten students. During the ranking discussion, explain that the strategies on the chart are also meant to help them practice and use resources on their own. Asking someone for an answer is not always possible, may disturb other students, and does not help students discover things for themselves. For these reasons, it should be last on the list of strategies.

Counting Words and Fold and Whisper

Overview

The Counting Words and Fold and Whisper techniques are multisensory strategies used together to help students plan, count, and write words to create sentences. The teacher leads students in finger counting the number of words in a sentence or phrase to be written, and then determines the words to be written next using Fold and Whisper.

Materials

- *Penmanship Oral Directions* (pages 20–21)

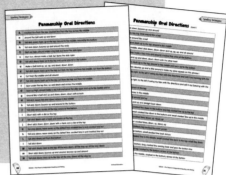

Procedure

1. Seat students around an easel with chart paper. Tell them, "We will be writing a sentence today. Sometimes, when we have to write a sentence, we forget what we want to write, and the words get lost. Let's practice a new way to write a sentence and stay on track."

2. Create a sentence using words from the word wall, sound chart, or anchor charts. For example, *I see a fish*. Say the sentence aloud, and have students repeat it.

3. Model holding one fist in the air and putting the other hand under your elbow for support. Say, "Watch what I do as I say our sentence." As you say the words, count them by raising one finger for each, starting with your index finger. Ask, "How many fingers do I have up?"

4. After a student responds correctly (four), say, "Now, it's time for you to try. Make a fist, and put your hand under your elbow." After all students have done this, continue by saying, "Repeat the sentence after me, and put up one finger every time we say a new word." Say the sentence several more times as students practice raising their fingers correctly.

5. Next say, "Now, count how many fingers you have up. Everyone tell me how many." After students respond, say, "If you said four fingers, you are correct. Four fingers means there are four words in our sentence."

6. Ask students, "What is the first word of the sentence?" (*I*). Demonstrate finding *I* on the word wall and writing it on the board while giving directions for the strokes using *Penmanship Oral Directions*. Have students echo the strokes.

7. As you model and describe the letter strokes, have a student helper write the *I* on the chart paper using Echo Writing (pages 18–19).

Counting Words and Fold and Whisper *(cont.)*

Procedure *(cont.)*

8. Say, "Good writers are good readers, and good readers are good writers, so we must read what we have written." Read the *I* with the class, and place the pointer/spacer on the easel or board after the *I*.

9. Have students make fists and put their hands under their elbows. Say the whole sentence with counting. Then, tell students they are going to fold their first fingers for *I* since it was written (*I*).

10. Next say, "Let's do it together." Fold and Whisper the sentence with students by whispering the word *I*, folding down the first finger for *I*, and saying the rest of the sentence.

11. Say, "What word do we need to write next? It is the word that comes after the one we whispered." (*see*) Continue the process, modeling the steps to add each word to the written sentence. Model using the word wall, sound chart, and other anchor charts in the room for spelling each word.

12. When the sentence is completed, Fold and Whisper the sentence with the class. Then ask, "What comes next in the sentence?" Acknowledge correct answers, and say, "Your fist will remind you that we have to end the sentence with a period. Your fist is the period!" Demonstrate writing a period on the small whiteboard, and ask one student to come make a period at the end of the sentence on the easel or board.

Cathy's Connections

Beginning writers often have misconceptions about punctuation and may need to be explicitly shown how to make punctuation marks. For example, when putting a period at the end of a sentence, you might say, "A period is a small dot at the end of a telling sentence. It belongs on the line. It is not a balloon or a big rock. It is a dot." Students will appreciate the humor, and you will have established a norm that you can refer to in future lessons.

4 to Score! Illustrations—Day 1

Overview

This lesson takes place over four days. Students create drawings that serve as examples and non-examples of illustration techniques. Beginning writers benefit from guided drawing and coloring practice that will enhance their independent illustrating efforts.

Materials

- *4 to Score! Poster* (page 55; see Digital Resources for a color version)
- picture books (a combination of books with realistic illustrations, such as *Hedgie's Surprise* by Jan Brett, and books with imaginative illustrations, such as *Duncan the Story Dragon* by Amanda Driscoll)

Preparation

Color the *4 to Score! Poster* if you are not using the color version. Leave the face in box one uncolored. Color the house in box two neatly. In box three, color the sun with a checkmark yellow and the sun with an *X* purple. Finally, in box four, color the heart with a checkmark neatly using a red crayon. Then, scribble on the heart with an *X* using the same red crayon.

Procedure

1. Gather students in front of the poster. Say, "Today, we are going to talk about illustrations. Some authors create pictures to go with their writing. These pictures are called illustrations."

2. Discuss with students why illustrations are important. Reinforce that they add details to help the reader understand the words. Hold up a picture book, and read the title and the names of the author and illustrator.

3. Read aloud a page from a book with realistic illustrations, and then ask students what they see in the illustrations that helps them better understand the words. After several students have responded, choose an image from the page and point out several details in it. Use the word *detail(s)* as you discuss the illustration. Ask, "Do you see details in the illustration that the author did not write about but that help us understand the story?"

4. Repeat Steps 2 and 3 with several other books so students can see a variety of illustrations.

5. Direct students' attention to the *4 to Score! Poster*. Tell them that *4 to Score* means that when they draw fantastic illustrations with details, it is like scoring a goal, home run, touchdown, or basket. Explain that they will learn more about what *4 to Score* means over the next few days.

6. Say, "We are authors. We can draw illustrations with details that will help readers understand our writing. Tomorrow, we will practice drawing illustrations!"

4 to Score! Poster

Draw with a pencil.

Color with crayons.

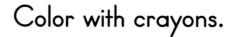

Color appropriately.

Color carefully.

4 to Score! Illustrations—Day 2

Materials

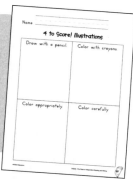

- *4 to Score! Illustrations* (page 57); replicate on a sheet of chart paper to make an anchor chart
- student copies of *4 to Score! Illustrations* (page 57)

Procedure

1. Seat students at their desks. Show them the *4 to Score! Illustrations* anchor chart, and invite them to read the title with you. Review the importance of illustrations and details to readers.

2. Say, "Today, you will practice making drawings with details. The tool you will be using is a pencil."

3. Discuss the benefits of using a pencil for drawing rather than crayons or markers.

4. Distribute copies of *4 to Score! Illustrations* to students.

5. Read aloud the directions in the top-left box. (1. Draw with a pencil.) Have students draw a simple illustration with some details using their pencils. (For example, students can draw a face or flower.) Draw on the anchor chart while students are working on their own papers. Ask one or two students to share their drawings and one detail they included. Compliment students on their drawings.

6. Next say, "Another way to add details to your illustrations is with color. Crayons are a tool we use to add color." Read aloud the directions in the top-right box. (2. Color with crayons.) Have students use their pencils to draw simple illustrations with details in box two, and then color them with crayons. Do the same on the anchor chart.

7. When students are finished, tell them to turn and share their details and coloring with partners. When they finish, say, "Adding colors will help your readers to see more details."

8. Save the anchor chart and student papers for Day 3.

Cathy's Connections

You can demonstrate for your students how using a pencil to draw and add details to a picture is more effective than using a crayon. Showing students how to use simple shapes to create images (a bus is a rectangle body with a square hood, a rectangle door with square windows, and circle tires), and then adding details, will help them successfully create detailed illustrations independently.

4 to Score! Illustrations

Draw with a pencil.	Color with crayons.
Color appropriately.	Color carefully.

4 to Score! Illustrations—Day 3

Materials

- 4 to Score! Illustrations anchor chart (from Day 2)
- student copies of *4 to Score! Illustrations* (from Day 2)
- picture book with realistic illustrations

Procedure

1. Begin Day 3 with students at their desks. Distribute the *4 to Score! Illustrations* student pages from Day 2. Say, "If you are illustrating a story, you should try to make sure that the illustrations make sense. Unless you are writing an imaginative story, you should color the pictures realistically."

2. Point to box three on the anchor chart, and read it aloud. (3. Color appropriately.) Tell students that they will draw two matching illustrations in the box. A sun is the perfect example for this exercise. Say, "We will be coloring one illustration realistically and the other in imaginative colors."

3. Explain to students that the word *realistic* means that the picture looks like the real thing. Show pages from a picture book with realistic illustrations of objects, such as trees, grass, flowers, or animals, and restate that these pictures are colored realistically.

4. Model drawing two suns on the anchor chart. Color one yellow and one purple. Discuss the imaginative drawing, asking what makes it unrealistic. Tell students to do the same using their own images. Have students share with partners what makes their imaginative drawings unrealistic.

5. On the anchor chart, model circling the realistically colored picture and putting a box around the imaginatively colored one. Have students do the same on their papers. Say, "Now you know two ways to color your illustrations."

6. Save the anchor chart and student papers for Day 4.

4 to Score! Illustrations—Day 4

Materials

- 4 to Score! Illustrations anchor chart (from Days 2 and 3)
- student copies of *4 to Score! Illustrations* (from Days 2 and 3)

Procedure

1. Seat students at their desks. Distribute the *4 to Score! Illustrations* student pages from Day 3. Have students help you retell the 4 to Score! steps.

2. Say, "We have practiced drawing with our pencils and coloring with our crayons. We have colored using realistic and imaginative colors. Today, we are going to practice coloring carefully and inside the lines."

3. Read aloud the fourth box. (*4. Color carefully.*) Ask, "What does it mean to color something carefully?" After reinforcing correct responses, have students draw two matching illustrations in the box. Ask them to color one of the pictures with realistic colors and inside the lines and one with scribbles. Complete the anchor chart as students work.

4. When students are finished, have one or two of them share their pictures with the class. Have students point out the differences between the carefully colored pictures and the scribbled pictures.

5. Finally, use the anchor chart to lead students in putting an *X* on their scribbled picture. Say, "Now you have your very own 4 to Score! anchor chart. When you follow these four steps, your illustrations will support your writing and help your readers."

Next Steps

Display the 4 to Score! Illustrations anchor chart in the classroom. For several weeks, review the chart before daily writing activities. Find illustrations in classroom books with examples of realistic and imaginative colors, and ask students to look closely at the illustrations for important details. Have students add their personal copies of 4 to Score! to their writing folders.

The Big 3—Day 1

Overview

This lesson takes place over five days. Students are introduced to three elements of sentence construction: beginning capitalization, spacing, and ending punctuation. The teacher practices "The Big 3" song and accompanying gestures with students and guides them to identify and edit the three elements in example sentences. During the week, the teacher creates an anchor chart with students.

Materials

• chart paper

Procedure

Note: As you create the Big 3 anchor chart, interactively write the sentences with students using these strategies: Stretch-a-Word (page 22), Counting Words and Fold and Whisper (pages 52–53), and Echo Writing (pages 18–19).

1. Say, "We are growing into readers and writers this year. Today, we will talk about writing sentences correctly. When we write a sentence correctly, it helps the reader understand what we are trying to say. We will make a chart to help us remember our rules as authors. In kindergarten, we have three rules. We are going to call them the *Big 3.*"

2. Continue by saying, "Let's put a title on our chart. This is an easy one because we are going to write the word *big,* and we know that word." Students can find the word on the word wall or other anchor charts in the room. Ask students to chant the spelling of *big.* Have one student write *Big* on the chart starting with a capital *B* because it is the title. Ask another student to write the number *3.*

The Big 3—Day 1 *(cont.)*

Procedure *(cont.)*

3. Under the title, write the number *1*. Say, "The first thing we need at the beginning of a sentence is a capital letter. Number 1 will say, *Start with a capital*. Let's count that on our fingers." Count, stretch, and write each word in the sentence. If the words *start* and *with* are on the word wall, one student should write the whole word. Write the word *capital* in a different color to show emphasis. After the first sentence, add the sentence, *No crazy capitals.*

4. Practice editing sentences that contain capitalization errors with the class. For example, *the dog is big.; the Dog is brown.;* and *the dog is in the Yard.* Introduce the editing mark of three lines under the letters that need capitalization and a slash over the letters that should not be capitalized.

5. To conclude the lesson, say, "The Big 3 is a great strategy to help make us successful authors. What did we practice today?" After students respond, say, "Yes. Today, we practiced making capital letters at the beginning of our sentences and looking for crazy capitals."

6. Save the Big 3 anchor chart for Day 2.

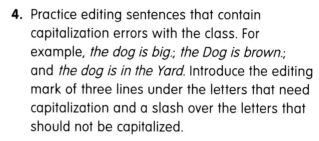

What Are Crazy Capitals?

When early learners begin writing, they need to be explicitly taught when and how to use capital letters. At first, this instruction focuses on starting names and sentences with capitals. Beginning writers tend to use capitals randomly, in the middle of words. Hunting for and identifying these "Crazy Capitals" is an engaging activity for students during shared writing and will transfer to their independent writing. When editing, lightly slash the incorrectly capitalized letters with a pencil, and teach students to erase the "Crazy Capitals" and fix their writing.

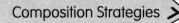

The Big 3—Day 2

Materials

- Big 3 anchor chart (from Day 1)
- sentence strips

Procedure

1. Say, "Yesterday, we started our Big 3 anchor chart. We added the title and the first rule of the Big 3. Who remembers the first rule of the Big 3?" Wait for student responses.

2. Continue by saying, "The first rule is to start a sentence with a capital letter. Today, we are going to add the second rule of the Big 3." Under the number *1*, write the number *2*. "We want to make sure that all the words in a sentence are separated so our writing can be read easily. For number 2, we are going to write, *Put in spaces.*" Interactively write the sentence on the anchor chart. Write *spaces* in a different color to show emphasis.

3. Practice editing sentences without spaces with the class. For the first example, write the sentence *I see the cat.* on a sentence strip, with a space missing between the words *I* and *see*. Once students determine where the space is missing in the sentence, draw a closed circle between the *I* and the *see*. Cut the sentence strip between the *I* and the *see*, and display it showing a space. Continue practicing with sentences on sentence strips in this manner. Include sentences that have more than one space missing.

4. After practicing several sentences, say, "Great job today putting spaces between the words in sentences. We are learning rules that help us to be great authors for our readers."

5. Save the Big 3 anchor chart for Day 3.

The Big 3—Day 3

Materials

- Big 3 anchor chart (from Days 1 and 2)

. . . .

Procedure

1. Say, "We have been working on our Big 3 anchor chart. We added the title and the first rule about capitals." Read number 1 with students. "We learned the second rule about spaces." Read number 2 with students. "Today, we are going to add one last rule about what happens at the end of sentences."

2. Lead students in a discussion about end marks. Include periods, question marks, and exclamation marks. Under the number *2,* write the number *3.* Interactively write the last sentence of the anchor chart: *End with an end mark.* Add all three types of end marks to the chart.

3. Practice putting periods in example sentences with the class. Model drawing a circle where a period should be and filling in the circle with the period.

4. Say, "We are going to be the best authors we can be by using this chart when we write sentences." Reread the anchor chart with the class.

5. Save the Big 3 anchor chart for Day 4.

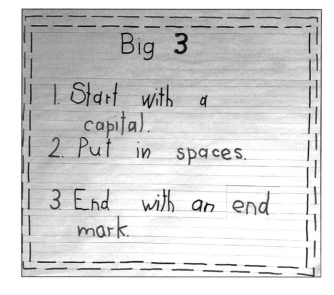

The Big 3—Day 4

Materials
- Big 3 anchor chart (from Days 1–3)
- chart paper

Procedure

1. Say, "This week, we have been learning how to write great sentences so that all readers can enjoy our writing. Let's review our chart." Review each element of the Big 3 anchor chart.

2. Write three sentences on a sheet of chart paper representing errors in punctuation rules from the Big 3 anchor chart. In the top corner of the chart paper, write a large *3*. Explain to students that the *3* has three points and represents the Big 3.

3. Correct the sentences with students. Reference the Big 3 anchor chart as you make the corrections. After you check for and correct capital letter errors, make a check on the top point of the *3*. Make a check on the middle point of the *3* after you check for and correct for spaces. Finally, check for and correct end marks, and then make a check on the bottom point of the *3*.

4. To conclude the lesson, say, "I am so excited about our new writing chart. This will help us write fantastic sentences."

5. Save the Big 3 anchor chart for Day 5.

Cathy's Connections

Although most students' sentences will use periods, they will need to master the use of other forms of punctuation at the ends of sentences. Provide opportunities daily for students to practice reading sentences with a variety of punctuation marks. Provide examples of a sentence written three times—once with a period, once with a question mark, and once with an exclamation mark. Ask students to read the sentences three ways. This is a great way to connect reading and writing in purposeful practice.

The Big 3—Day 5

Materials

- Big 3 anchor chart (from Days 1–4)
- *"Big 3 Song"* (page 66)

Procedure

1. Reread the anchor chart with the class. Say, "Now, I'm going to teach you a song to help us remember our rules for the Big 3."

2. Teach students the "Big 3 Song" and accompanying gestures.

3. Write *I see the dog.* on the board. Say, "Let's use what we've learned about making sentences from our song to see if this sentence is correct." Ask students to identify the Big 3 in the sentence. As they identify the three elements, underline the capital letter at the beginning three times, and draw closed circles to identify the spaces between the words. As you circle the period, say, "A telling sentence ends with a period."

4. To conclude the lesson, say, "The Big 3 are a great way to help us be successful authors. We are making sure to write what we want in a way that helps our readers understand. When you are writing, the 'Big 3 Song' can help you."

Continue to practice writing sentences. As you do, use three lines under a capital, a closed circle to show spaces between words, and a circle around the end mark. These proofreading marks will help students remember and apply the rules.

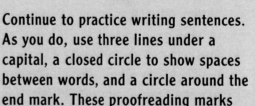

Next Steps

A *Big 3 Weekly Rubric* is included with the Digital Resources. It can be a helpful tool for students and parents. The rubric is printed on the right half of a sheet of paper so it can be folded around several pages of handwriting paper to create a Big 3 journal. As students finish their writing each day, use the rubric to make sure they have completed their sentences correctly. Reviewing the rubric from their previous day's writing will remind them of any areas that need improvement.

Big 3 Song

(sung to the tune of "Baa, Baa, Black Sheep")

Writing a sentence is easy as can be. (*Hold out one hand like a tablet, and pretend to write with the index finger of the other hand on the tablet.*)

All you need are the Big 3. (*Hold up 3 fingers.*)

Start with a capital. (*Hold both arms straight up beside your ears to stretch up tall.*)

Put spaces in between. (*Hold hands near shoulders with palms facing out. Pulse arms in and out to create a space.*)

End with an end mark. (*Hold one hand open, and pound the fist of the other hand into the open hand.*)

Keeps it nice and clean. (*Nod your head up and down.*)

Writing a sentence is easy as can be. (*Hold out one hand like a tablet, and pretend to write with the index finger of the other hand on the tablet.*)

All you need are the Big 3. (*Hold up 3 fingers.*)

Build-a-Sentence

Overview

This lesson takes place over four days. Students practice reading sight words and combining them with picture word cards to make predictable sentences. After creating sentences with the cards, students write sentences using the models.

Materials

- chart paper with the title "Build-a-Sentence"
- *Build-a-Sentence Word Cards* (page 70; see Digital Resources for a color version); cut apart the cards; use one sentence a day for four days

Procedure

1. Gather students together on the carpet. Show students the *Build-a-Sentence Word Cards* for the first sentence, *We see the dip.* Say, "Today, we will be writing a sentence. We will use these cards to make the sentence." Read aloud the words on the cards with students.

2. Rearrange the cards so they are out of order, and read the sentence out loud. Ask, "Does that make sense?" After acknowledging student responses, say, "Let me read them again." Rearrange the words again so they are still out of order. "I don't think that makes sense either. I know it has to make sense and sound right. When I read, 'see the We dip,' it doesn't make sense, and it doesn't sound right. What can I do to make this right?"

3. When a student says the words need to be moved around, say, "Yes, let's rearrange the words and see if they will make sense. I'm going to need help."

4. Ask for four volunteers to hold one word card each. As the volunteers line up, have the rest of the class read the sentence aloud. Rearrange the words to make nonsense sentences, asking students if the sentences are correct.

5. Once students have determined the order that sounds right and makes sense, tape the cards in the correct order on the chart paper. Say, "This sentence sounds amazing. Let's write it."

6. Use interactive writing to have students help write the sentence on the chart.

7. After the sentence is written, say, "I am excited! We have just created a sentence that makes sense and sounds right. We made a fantastic sentence today."

8. Save the Build-a-Sentence anchor chart for Days 2 through 4.

9. For Days 2 through 4, lead students in the steps above to write the following sentences:
   - Day 2—We see the clip.
   - Day 3—We see the chip.
   - Day 4—We see the ship.

10. Each day, have students read the previously written sentences. By the fourth day, students should discover that the last words in the sentences rhyme. Highlight or circle the four rhyming words, and discuss the pattern.

Build-a-Sentence (cont.)

Cathy's Connections

Early writers benefit from constructing and writing predictable sentences. As you model writing these sentences, reinforce the Big 3 (pages 60–66).

Build-a-Sentence Center

Students will independently write predictable sentences. Use the sentences from the group lesson the first time this activity is included in the center rotation. Students will not have written the sentences independently, and providing this example and review will serve as a successful scaffold for them.

Materials

- *Build-a-Sentence Writing Paper* (page 69)
- *Build-a-Sentence Student Word Cards* (page 71; see Digital Resources for a color version)

Activities

Introduce this center after teaching the *Build-a-Sentence* (page 67–71) lesson and practicing with several other simple sentences.

Show students the materials for this center. Demonstrate how to cut apart the cards, make sentences, and write the sentences.

- Work together to create an anchor chart that shows the steps.
  1. Cut apart the words and read them.
  2. Make sentences with the cards.
  3. Glue the words down.
  4. Write the sentences under the cards.

- Continue developing independent writing skills in this center throughout the year, using different sight words and word cards.
- Rotate other word and picture cards into this center for additional practice.
- Support students struggling to complete this center independently by writing the sentence starter on a sentence strip.

Name _____

Build-a-Sentence Writing Paper

Directions: Build a sentence. Write the words.

Build-a-Sentence Word Cards

We | see | the |
dip | .

We | see | the | clip | .

We | see | the | chip | .

We | see | the |
ship | .

Build-a-Sentence Student Word Cards

the	dip	We	see
see	We	clip	the
chip	the	see	We
We	ship	the	see

the	dip	We	see
see	We	clip	the
chip	the	see	We
We	ship	the	see

124548—The Road to Independent Reading and Writing

Predictable Sentences

Overview

Writing predictable sentences serves as an important scaffold for early learners for sentence structure, spelling, and punctuation. This lesson begins with whole-class instruction in writing predictable sentences. Students will then independently create predictable sentences in their writing journals.

Materials

- *Sentence Starters* (page 74); cut apart
- lined writing paper

Procedure

1. Gather students around an easel with chart paper. Say, "Today, we are going to write sentences. I have sentence starters that will help us. Let's pull one out and use it to write a sentence." Hold out the sentence starters, and have a student choose one. Help the student read it to the class.

2. Next, ask a student to choose a word from the sound chart or picture cards to complete the sentence. State the complete sentence for students using the chosen word. Have students recite the sentence orally several times.

3. Select several students to help write the sentence on the board. Incorporate strategies such as Counting Words and Fold and Whisper (pages 52–53) as you guide students.

4. Review the completed sentence using the Big 3 strategy (pages 60–66). Ask students questions, such as "How do you start a sentence? What do you put between words? How do you end a telling sentence?"

5. Ask students to create a new sentence using the same sentence starter and choosing a new word from the sound chart or picture cards to complete the sentence. Have students tell their new sentences to partners. Monitor their conversations to make sure they are saying complete sentences. When they are finished, ask for a few student volunteers to share their new sentences.

6. Say, "Now that we have practiced making sentences, you can write them all by yourselves!" Have students return to their seats. Distribute lined writing paper to students.

> Using a pocket chart during interactive writing allows for storing and displaying sentence strips, such as *Sentence Starters* (page 74). The *Sound Chart* (page 17) can also be enlarged and cut apart to create individual picture word cards that students will be familiar with and can use to construct sentences.

Predictable Sentences (cont.)

Procedure (cont.)

7. Practice the sentence starter again orally. Tell each student to insert his or her own word at the end of the sentence. Review sentence capitalization and punctuation using the Big 3 anchor chart. Have students write their new sentences on their papers.

8. Rotate around the room, checking in with students as they complete their first sentences. Then, have students write two more sentences using the same sentence starter. Continue circulating and monitoring for penmanship, spelling, and sentence mechanics.

Next Steps

Repeat the lesson using other sentence starters. Once a sentence starter has been introduced, add it to the word wall. Encourage students to use the sentence starters when they journal. When the process becomes routine, students can use other words in their sentences, such as seasonal words or words from books. See Digital Resources for *Seasonal Word Cards*.

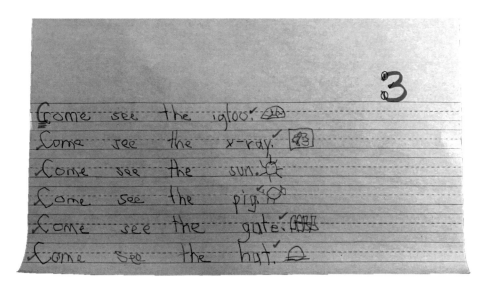

Cathy's Connections

If we take the fear out of writing, students will write forever. Part of what we need to do with early writers is teach them to enjoy writing. Eliminating fears of "spelling it wrong" or "making mistakes" creates students who not only *will* write, but will write *a lot*.

I see the

Look at the

Here is the

I can see a

I like the

Four-Square Target Writing—Day 1

Overview

Students are introduced to a graphic organizer through a week-long, cumulative lesson. The graphic organizer is used to independently plan paragraphs with a main idea and four supporting details or sequence of events.

Materials

- *Four-Square Target Farm Example* (page 76; see Digital Resources for a color version)

Procedure

1. Display *Four-Square Target Farm Example.* Say, "Let me show you a tool we will use this year to help us write. First, what is a tool?" After students respond, say, "A tool is something you use to help you do a job. This is a writing tool. It is called a *Four-Square Target* because it helps us stay on target with a topic. This one is filled out, and the topic is in the middle of the page." Point to the topic box, and say, "Let me read it to you: *A Day on the Farm.*"

2. Ask students, "What will this story be about?" Affirm students by saying, "That's right, the topic of this story is a farm. Let's write our own topic sentence using some of the words on the page. If you went to visit a farm and you wanted to write about it, your topic sentence could be *I went to the farm one day.*"

3. Lead the class in an interactive writing experience to record the topic sentence on a sheet of chart paper. Use strategies such as Echo Writing (pages 18–19) and Counting Words and Fold and Whisper (pages 52–53) to help individual students write the words for the sentence. Model using Stretch-a-Word (page 22) and the Big 3 (pages 60–66) if needed.

4. When the sentence is completed, say, "What a great start to our story about a day on the farm. Let's look at the Four-Square Target. What are we going to write about tomorrow?"

5. After acknowledging student responses, reinforce the importance of starting in the top-left corner of the Four-Square Target. Remind students by saying, "We always read and write from left to right and from the top of the page, not the bottom."

6. Save the writing chart for Day 2.

> Beginning readers and writers will have difficulty identifying or creating topic sentences. They may consistently confuse details with topics. For this reason, model the topic sentence the first few times you practice Four-Square Target writing with the class, and gradually begin asking them for topic sentences. When they respond with details, specifically point out that they are details about the topic, not the topic itself.

Four-Square Target Farm Example

farmer

barn

A Day on the Farm

hay

tractor

Four-Square Target Writing—Day 2

Materials

- *Four-Square Target Farm Example* (page 76; see Digital Resources for a color version)
- writing chart (from Day 1)

Procedure

1. Return to the chart with the topic sentence from yesterday. Say, "Yesterday, we started using a new writing tool. What is it called?" Acknowledge correct answers and say, "That's right, it's a Four-Square Target. We used the topic box yesterday to write our topic sentence. Let's reread it." Point to the words on the chart paper as the class reads the sentence you wrote together yesterday.

2. Review the Four-Square Target writing tool, and discuss the top-left corner of the chart. Ask students what they see in the picture and what they think the word says. Ask, "Might you see a farmer if you went to visit a farm?" After they respond, say, "A farmer is a detail you could write about."

3. Work with students to create a sentence about the farmer. If you want to use predictable sentences, you could suggest phrases, such as *I see the____*, *Here is the____*, or *Look at the____*. If you want to focus on telling a story, lead students toward an introductory sentence, such as *We saw a farmer*.

4. Lead the class in an interactive writing experience to record the sentence on the chart paper.

5. Complete the lesson by saying, "Great job! Let's check out tomorrow's square and think of what we are going to write." Select two students to give sentence examples. Then say, "Please turn to your neighbor and share a sentence idea for tomorrow."

6. Save the writing chart for Day 3.

The anchor chart that you are creating with the class is intended to be displayed in the classroom as an anchor chart for students to use as a resource. All words should be spelled correctly. A long discussion about the spelling of each word is not necessary, but spelling rules should be acknowledged. For example, if students want to spell the word *road*, sound the /r/ at the beginning and the long /o/ in the middle. You can give a short explanation by saying "a long vowel sound can be spelled differently. In this word, the long *o* sound is spelled *oa*, even though we don't hear the *a* at all." Finish the word by sounding the /d/ at the end.

Four-Square Target Writing—Days 3–5

Materials

- *Four-Square Target Farm Example* (page 76; see Digital Resources for a color version)
- writing chart (from Days 1 and 2)
- prewritten or pretyped sentences from the chart paper

Procedure

1. Begin each day by reviewing the previous days' writing. Remind students by saying, "Good readers are good writers, and good writers are good readers."

2. Use interactive writing to have students help record the remaining sentences on the chart paper. Record one sentence per day. Create sentences using the words from the remaining Four-Square Target boxes (*barn, hay, tractor*).

3. On Day 5, read the entire piece with the class. Say, "I am very proud of our writing this week. We have used a new tool for writing sentences and telling a story. We're going to create another story using our new writing tool next week, and soon, you will be using it on your own to write stories."

4. Write or type the sentences from the chart paper onto a sheet of paper, leaving space for a drawing. Distribute copies of the completed papers to students for them to illustrate and keep to practice reading. Display the *Four-Square Target Farm Example* and the completed story as an anchor chart.

Next Steps

After at least two shared writing experiences with the Four-Square Target and other topics, students can start using the organizer independently. Take the time to specifically identify the template as a prewriting resource, and make it available for students when they write. Periodically share different examples of how students use the organizer. As they master a topic sentence and four detail sentences, demonstrate including two details in each box and writing two sentences for each, or demonstrate creating more complicated sentences. (*I went to the barn. It was red.* Or, *I went to the red barn.*)

Four-Square Target Writing—Days 3-5 (cont.)

Cathy's Connections

This technique was developed by Judith Gould and Evan Gould, and I think it is misunderstood. It is a plan of what a student wants to write. I introduce Four-Square Target as a plan for a story, but it isn't the story. I especially like using it with my struggling writers because it allows for early success.

Once students are independently using Four-Square Target for writing, provide individual instruction about adding details. If the first box shows leaves, students could add sentences about raking the leaves. (I see the leaves. I can rake the leaves.) Students could be encouraged to write about the color, size, or location. Students' stories will expand, as will their confidence in writing.

Seeing your students achieve independence in writing is a great moment! It's also one of the most valuable lessons they need to move on to first grade, and it isn't hard. Start a routine with writing, and they can write about anything. Students are only limited by the lessons they don't learn. Using the Four-Square Target can help each child progress at his or her own pace and level. It's the perfect differentiation tool.

Four-Square Target Writing Center

Using *Four-Square Writing,* students independently write at least four sentences on a topic.

Materials

- writing paper
- student copies of *Four-Square Writing* (page 80)
- *Four-Square Target Farm Example* (page 76; see Digital Resources for a color version)

Activities

Introduce this center after the week-long Four-Square Target Writing lessons. Display the anchor chart from the lesson at the center for student reference as well as the *Four-Square Target Farm Example* (page 76).

- Include vocabulary cards, such as *Seasonal Word Cards* (available in Digital Resources).
- Encourage students writing independently to create their own topics, frames, and sentences.
- Support struggling students by numbering each of the boxes on the Four-Square Writing template so they know in which order to write the sentences. A sentence strip with a sentence starter can also be provided as additional support.
- Provide scaffolding to struggling writers by completing the *Four-Square Writing* for students.

Name _____

Four-Square Writing

Directions: Write a topic. Draw four details.

First, Then, Last—Day 1

Overview

Sequencing is an essential skill for success in writing and reading. Students practice their sequencing and writing skills during this three-day, whole-group activity by ordering a three-part picture puzzle, creating sentences to describe the pictures, and using signal words (*first, then, last*) to describe the order.

Materials

- *Three-Part Puzzle* (page 82; see Digital Resources for a color version); cut apart

Procedure

1. Show students the puzzle pieces out of order and not connected. Say, "We have been reading stories and discussing the sequencing of the stories. Today, we are going to start writing our own stories using the sequencing words: *first, then,* and *last.*"

2. Discuss the pictures on each piece of the puzzle with the class. Model how to describe the details and action shown on the first puzzle piece. Then, have students turn and talk with partners to describe the second and third pieces. Call on student volunteers to share details or actions from the other two pieces.

3. Guide the class in a discussion of how the pieces should go together, from first to last. Put the pieces in the correct order. Ask students why the pieces only fit together in one order.

4. Say, "We aren't going to write today. We have talked about how writing involves planning time. Today, we made our plan. We have told the story in the correct sequence. Tomorrow, we will start writing our story."

Three-Part Puzzle

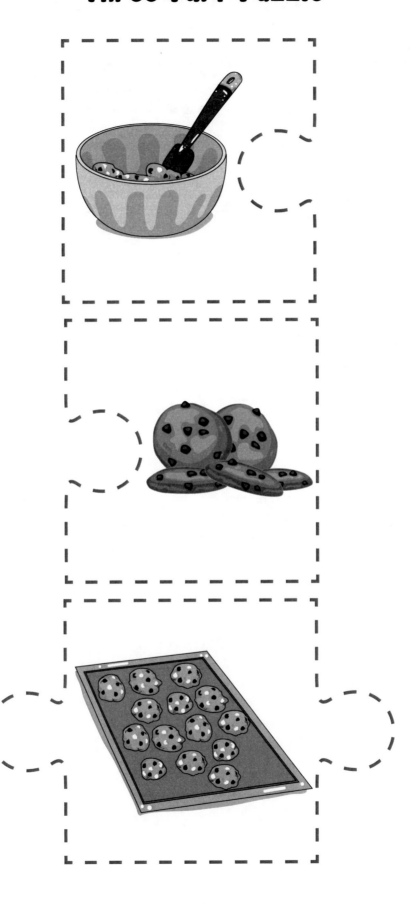

First, Then, Last—Day 2

Materials

- *Three-Part Puzzle* (page 82; see Digital Resources for a color version); cut apart
- sentence strips

Procedure

1. Gather students so they can all see the displayed puzzle pieces from yesterday's lesson. Begin the lesson with the pieces out of order and not connected. Say, "Yesterday, we made a plan for a story using our puzzle pieces. What comes first? Then what happens? What comes last?"

2. Assemble the pieces in the correct order according to student responses. Say, "Great job. Today, we will write the first sentence. We will start the sentence with the signal word *First.* There are other signal words for starting a sequenced story, but today, we will use *First.*"

3. Summarize student responses from yesterday into three simple sentences using the signal words *First, Then,* and *Last.* For example: *First, the children mix the cookies. Then, they bake the cookies. Last, the cookies are done.* Say the sentences in order, pointing to the puzzle pieces, and have students echo each sentence.

4. Use interactive writing and *Counting Words and Fold and Whisper* (pages 52–53) to have students help record the first sentence on a sheet of chart paper. Use the word wall or Stretch-a-Word (page 22) to spell *First* and any other difficult words.

5. When you are finished with the first sentence, read it again with the class, and say, "We did a wonderful job starting our story. Tomorrow, we will add the sentence about what happens *next* or *then.*"

6. Save the chart with the sentence for Day 3.

Cathy's Connections

To help facilitate signal word use, prewrite *First, Then,* and *Last* on sentence strips. At this point of instruction, it is not necessary to spend extra time reviewing the use of the signal words. Rather, place instructional emphasis on correctly sequencing the story events and rereading the story to cement the *use* of signal words in students' writing experiences.

First, Then, Last—Day 3

Materials

- chart with sentence (from Day 2)
- *Three-Part Puzzle* (page 82; see Digital Resources for a color version); cut apart

Procedure

1. Begin by showing students the story puzzle pieces out of order. Say, "Do you remember the correct sequence of our story?" With class input, correctly sequence the puzzle pieces, reread the first sentence, and decide upon the second sentence. Interactively write the second sentence starting with *Then*. Use the word wall or Stretch-a-Word (page 22) to spell *Then* and any other difficult words and use Counting Words and Fold and Whisper (pages 52–53) to write the sentence.

2. Reread the sentences with the class. Next, say, "Close your eyes as I read the first two sentences of the story. As I read them, try to see what is happening first and then what is happening after that." Read the sentences to students.

3. Have students open their eyes, and ask, "Did you see what was happening in the story? What happened first? Then what happened?" After listening to student responses, say, "Tomorrow, we will finish our story."

4. Save the chart with the sentences for Day 4.

First, Then, Last—Day 4

Materials
- chart with sentences (from Days 2 and 3)
- *Three-Part Puzzle* (page 82; see Digital Resources for a color version); cut apart

Procedure

1. Before beginning the lesson, display the puzzle pieces in a mixed-up order. Begin the lesson by rereading the first two sentences of the story with the class. Ask, "Do the puzzle pieces match our story? Are they in the correct order?" Choose student volunteers to put the pieces in the correct order and justify their decisions by referring to the written story.

2. Compose the third sentence with the class using interactive writing and guide students to begin the sentence with *Last*. Use the word wall or Stretch-a-Word (page 22) to spell *Last* and any other difficult words. Ask students what the signal word is in this sentence. After acknowledging correct answers, say, "Adding *Last* to our sentence helps the reader understand the order of the story."

3. Reread the entire story with the class. Say, "I think this is a masterpiece. I can understand the story, and I can play it in my head like a movie. The signal words *First*, *Then*, and *Last*, help me understand the sequence of the story."

4. Save the chart with the sentences for Day 5.

After the Day 4 lesson, write or type the story on *Three-Part Puzzle Story* (page 88) to prepare for the Day 5 lesson.

First, Then, Last—Day 5

Materials

- chart with writing (from Days 2–4)
- student copies of *Three-Part Puzzle Story* (page 88); write or type the story written on Days 2–4 at the bottom before making copies

Procedure

1. Gather students around the chart with the completed story. Say, "This week, we wrote a story using sequencing and signal words. I want you to listen for the signal words as we read our story together."

2. Reread the completed story with the class. Ask, "What are the signal words?" After acknowledging correct responses (*First*, *Then*, *Last*), continue by saying, "I'm excited to share your story with you. Let's go back to our tables, and I have something to pass out to you."

3. Distribute copies of *Three-Part Puzzle Story* to students.

4. Read the story chorally with the class, having them point to the words as they read. Experiment with different ways of reading. For example, students can whisper or shout the signal words and the word *cookies*. Divide the class into thirds, and have each third read a sentence out loud. In groups of three, students can take turns reading one of the three sentences.

5. Have students illustrate the story. Remind them to correctly sequence the three illustrations, and have a brief discussion about the details they can draw in each section to help the reader understand each part of the story.

Next Steps

Follow this plan using different puzzles for three consecutive weeks so students are completely familiar with sequencing three pictures and can identify the signal words. Hang the story in the classroom so students can refer to it. Using this strategy, students can write *First*, *Then*, and *Last* sentences with success even before they have mastered sequencing.

First, Then, Last—Day 5 (cont.)

First, Then, Last Center

Students put sequencing puzzles in the correct order and write sentences to accompany them that begin with the signal words *First, Then,* and *Last*.

Materials

- student copies of *Three-Part Puzzle Story* (page 88)

Activities

It is important that introducing this center follows three weeks of whole-group practice in sequencing events and using the three signal words (*First, Then, Last*) to write about the events.

- Provide copies of *Three-Part Puzzle Story* for independent practice.

- Ensure students know where to find *First, Then,* and *Last* on the word wall.

- Review spelling strategies, such as Stretch-a-Word (page 22), Stoplight Writing (page 37–41), Think of a Word You Already Know (pages 42–44), and Use Resources to Find Words (pages 45–48) (in the room, in a book, or ask a friend or grown-up).

Name _____

Three-Part Puzzle Story

Directions: Draw pictures to match the story.

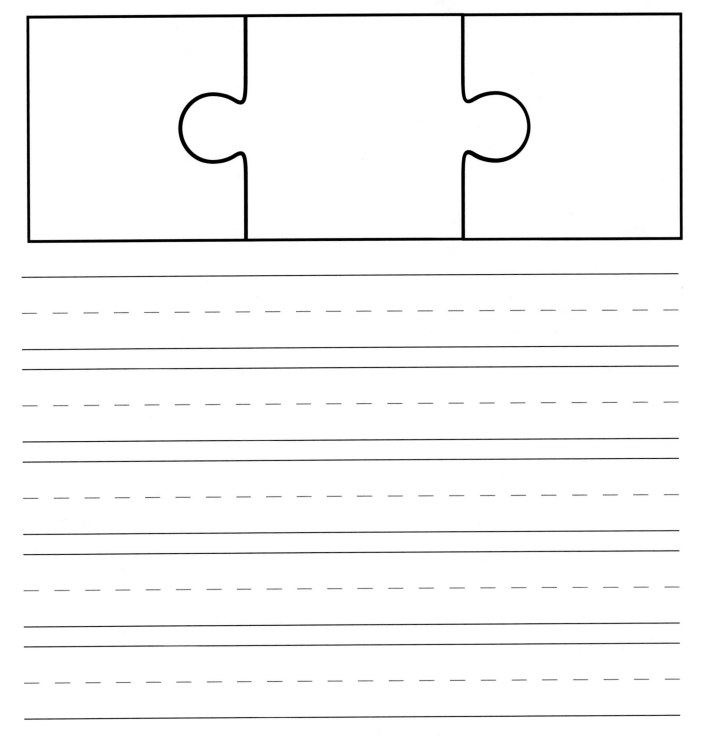

Sentence Maker—Day 1

Overview

This five-day lesson begins the second week of school. Students will use graphic organizers to write complete sentences. Students participate in a shared writing experience to create a four-sentence descriptive paragraph to serve as a model for independent writing.

Materials

- *Sentence Maker* (page 91; see Digital Resources for patterns to create a poster-size version)
- spacer

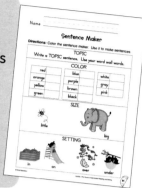

Procedure

1. Gather students on the carpet, and display the enlarged *Sentence Maker* and a sheet of chart paper. Tell students that they are going to become authors and write a story together using the *Sentence Maker*.

2. Point to the *Sentence Maker*. Say, "I have a tool that will help us write our story. This is called the Sentence Maker. Let's look at this tool." Point to the Topic box, and say, "The top box says *Topic*. A lot of students take the bus to school, and we have been reading about buses, so today, let's write about a bus. The topic is what our story will be about. Our story will be about a bus, so our topic is *bus*." Continue pointing to the Topic box, and ask, "Isn't it great that the <u>TOP</u>ic goes on the TOP?"

3. Point to the first box on the *Sentence Maker*. Say, "This says, 'Use your word wall words.' Let's look at the word wall and the phrase we made this week." Guide selected students to find the words *I*, *see*, and *a* on the word wall. Say, "Who remembers where our phrases are? A phrase is what we get when we put words together." Choose a student volunteer to point out the phrases on the word wall.

4. Say, "Good. *I see a.* Can we make a sentence about a bus using the phrase *I see a*? What would the sentence be?" Acknowledge a student who answers correctly, and say, "You are right, *I see a bus.*" Use Counting Words (pages 52–53) to identify and count the words in the sentence.

5. Identify with students that *I* is the first word in the sentence. Choose a student volunteer to come to the chart paper. Use Echo Writing (pages 18–19) to write the word *I*. If possible, choose someone whose first name begins with an *I*, and mention this to the class.

Sentence Maker—Day 1 *(cont.)*

6. After the student has written *I*, have the class read the word together, and tell them, "Good readers are good writers, and good writers are good readers, so we always read what we write." Then, point to the *I*, and put the pointer/spacer after it on the easel or magnetic board.

7. Continue writing the sentence with students, determining the next words to write using Counting Words and Fold and Whisper (pages 52–53) and spelling them using Echo Writing (pages 18–19). Have students write entire words instead of single letters to help establish words as units. If the word *bus* is not on your word wall, use the Stretch-a-Word (page 22) to spell it.

8. After completing the sentence, reread the entire sentence using Fold and Whisper. Point out that all their fingers have been folded down, and they have made a fist. Ask, "What comes at the end of a telling sentence? Look at your hand. What does it look like?" Students should respond that it looks like a period.

9. Reread the whole sentence one last time with the class. Say, "We have just finished the first sentence. We are on our way to writing a great story."

10. Save the *Sentence Maker* and writing chart for Day 2.

> Have students practice writing in the air, on their legs, or on the carpet with their fingers when you are modeling letter formation. Focusing on following the letter formation directions helps increase students' attention during the lesson.

Name _____

Sentence Maker

Directions: Color the sentence maker. Use it to make sentences.

TOPIC
Write a TOPIC sentence. Use your word wall words.

COLOR

red		blue		white	
orange		purple		gray	
yellow		brown		pink	
green		black			

SIZE

little

big

SETTING

in   on   over   under

Sentence Maker—Day 2

Materials

- *Sentence Maker* (from Day 1)
- writing chart (from Day 1)

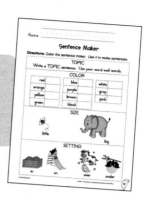

Procedure

1. Say to the class, "Yesterday, we wrote our first sentence. What was our topic? Where does the topic belong? What was the sentence all about?" Continue after a student has volunteered the topic *bus*, and say, "That's right! We wrote about a bus!" Ask for a volunteer to read the topic sentence.

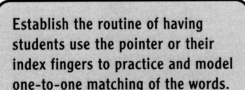

Establish the routine of having students use the pointer or their index fingers to practice and model one-to-one matching of the words.

2. Tell the class, "Today, we are going to write a new sentence to tell a reader what our bus looks like. Yesterday, we wrote about the topic." Point to the second section on the *Sentence Maker*, and say, "We are going to write about the color. What color are the buses here at school?" After a student gives the correct response, say, "Let's use the resources in the room to help us write *The bus is yellow*."

3. Use Counting Words (pages 52–53) to determine what the first word is. Continue by saying, "We have *the* on the word wall." Ask a student volunteer to get up and point to *the* on the word wall.

4. Follow the procedures for shouting the word, spelling, and modeling letter formation with Echo Writing (pages 18–19), and guide a student volunteer to write the word *The* from the word wall. Because *The* is at the beginning of the sentence, point out that it will begin with a capital *T*.

5. Continue writing the rest of the sentence using Counting Words and Fold and Whisper (pages 52–53) and Echo Writing. When you get to the word *yellow*, ask students, "Where can we find the color words in the room?" (on the color chart or Sentence Maker anchor chart). Work with students to determine the end mark.

6. Choral read the whole story starting with the title.

7. Preview the *Sentence Maker* for the next day. Say, "Tomorrow, we will be talking about our bus and what size it is. I want you to be thinking about if our bus is big or little."

8. Save the *Sentence Maker* and writing chart for Day 3.

Sentence Maker—Day 2 *(cont.)*

Cathy's Connections

Use previously written words and sentences to help students problem solve what to do in new writings. For example, when deciding how to begin the Day 2 sentence, use the Day 1 writing:

"Yesterday, when I wrote the sentence *I see a bus*, what kind of letter did we use at the beginning of the sentence? Did we use an uppercase *I* or a lowercase *i*? Right, it was an uppercase *I*. How do you think we should start the beginning of our new word? Yes, we should write a capital *T*."

Sentence Maker—Day 3

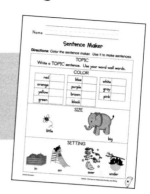

Materials

- *Sentence Maker* (from Days 1 and 2)
- writing chart (from Days 1 and 2)

Procedure

1. Tell students, "This week, we have been writing about a bus, and we have used the Sentence Maker to help us write our sentences. Let's read what we have already written so we can remember our story. We do this because good readers are good writers and good writers are good readers." Using the pointer/spacer, reread the first two sentences on the easel or board.

2. Point to the next line of the *Sentence Maker*. Say, "Today, we are going to write more about the bus. I asked you to think about our bus yesterday. This part of our Sentence Maker is about the size of the bus." Ask for volunteers to say sentences that include the size of the bus. Ask students why they think it is big or little. For example: *It is big because it is like the bus we ride to school*; *It is little because it is like the bus in my toy box.*

3. Work with students to determine what sentence the class will write. Say, "Our sentence will be *The bus is big.*" Use Counting Words (pages 52–53) to have students count the words in the sentence. Then, write the sentence with students using Fold and Whisper (pages 52–53) and Echo Writing (pages 18–19). Remind students to use the word *big* from the Sentence Maker anchor chart.

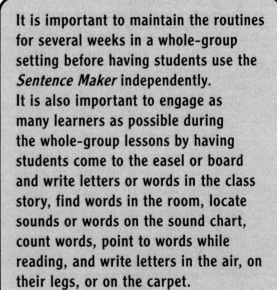

It is important to maintain the routines for several weeks in a whole-group setting before having students use the *Sentence Maker* independently. It is also important to engage as many learners as possible during the whole-group lessons by having students come to the easel or board and write letters or words in the class story, find words in the room, locate sounds or words on the sound chart, count words, point to words while reading, and write letters in the air, on their legs, or on the carpet.

4. Conclude the lesson by saying, "This is going to be the best story about a bus. I am very proud of us so far. Tomorrow, we will finish our story. We're going to tell where our bus is. This is called the setting of the story. Turn and talk for a minute about where you think our bus is going to be for tomorrow's sentence." Elicit responses from as many partners as possible before completing the lesson.

5. Save the *Sentence Maker* and writing chart for Day 4.

Sentence Maker—Day 4

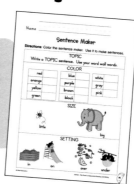

Materials

- *Sentence Maker* (from Days 1–3)
- writing chart (from Days 1–3)
- any children's storybook with pictures

Procedure

1. Review the previously written sentences with the class. Tell students the final sentence on the chart is about the setting. Ask students where they would find a bus. Allow several students to answer.

2. Direct students' attention to the *Sentence Maker*. Say, "Our chart gives us four ideas for where our story setting can be. Let's think of some ideas using the words *in, on, over*, and *under*." Look for responses such as *on the road, on the street, in my neighborhood, in the garage, under the tree, under the clouds, over the puddle*. Acknowledge all responses, but initially, choose a sentence with words that are easily decoded or can be written quickly. While *neighborhood* is a great answer, it's long and takes a lot of explanation.

3. Once you choose a sentence, have students count the words on their fingers. They will need to use two hands for this sentence.

4. All the words for this sentence should be on the chart except for the last word in the sentence. When you get to that word, guide the class through Stretch-a-Word (page 22) or another strategy to discern the correct spelling, but don't teach a lesson about it at this time.

5. Reread the whole story with the class.

6. Ask students to turn to partners, shake hands, and say, *Good job. Now YOU are an author!* Then, have them turn to another friend and do it again.

7. Conclude Day 4 by saying, "I am so proud of our story. I wonder what we are going to do tomorrow. Let's think about this. What else do we need? We have a title, and we have a story. Let's look at books to see what else we need."

8. Using a book, point to the title, and find the title on the class story. Then, point to the words in the book and the words in the class story. Next, point to an illustration in the book, and snap your fingers like you have an idea. Smile, nod your head, and tell them you know what's missing, and they'll have to wait until tomorrow to see what they have left to do.

9. Save the *Sentence Maker* and writing chart for Day 5.

> After the Day 4 lesson, type the story on one page in double-spaced large font with space at the top or bottom for an illustration. Include the title and a place for the author's name.

Sentence Maker—Day 4 *(cont.)*

Cathy's Connections

Don't be afraid to have fun with your class! Using humorous non-examples will help students remember to focus on real settings and will keep them engaged in the lesson. For example, ask, "Would we find a bus on the beach? Would we see a bus in a fish tank?"

Thinking aloud about new activities will also encourage students to try them without fear. For example, when counting a sentence using two hands for the first time, say, "We just counted six words! We haven't written one that long before. Do you think we can do it? Let's count it again to make sure."

Sentence Maker—Day 5

Materials

- *Sentence Maker* (from Days 1–4)
- writing chart (from Days 1–4)
- copies of typed story (from Day 4)
- any children's storybook with pictures

Procedure

1. Gather students together on the carpet for this celebration day. Distribute copies of the story to students, and read it aloud together.

2. Ask students to find the color word, the size word, and to identify the punctuation for the telling sentences.

3. Have students partner-read the story.

4. Discuss with the class ways to illustrate the story. Demonstrate how to draw a bus using shapes. Start with a large rectangle in the middle of the paper, adding a square to the front for the engine. Add circles for wheels, squares for windows, and a tall rectangle for the door. Once the wheels are on the bus, students can add a road underneath, lights, a bus number, and other details.

Students can add their stories to an author book. Punching holes in the papers and inserting them in a three-ring binder is an easy way to compile the stories. This becomes a perfect resource for independent reading.

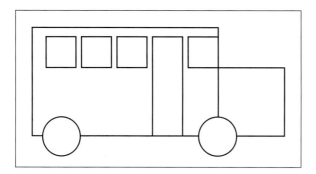

Sentence Maker—Day 5 *(cont.)*

Next Steps

Continue whole-group lessons with the *Sentence Maker* each week for the first few months of the school year. When they are ready, introduce students to their own independent writing folders. Initially, establish the daily routine of writing one sentence per day. Students will get in the habit of taking out their papers, writing a little, and putting their writing back in the folders appropriately. After a month of this routine, teach the What to Write About lesson (pages 99–102) to give students a strategy for choosing their own topics.

Cathy's Connections

When students have become proficient in using the *Sentence Maker* both as a class and independently, provide them with the *Sentence Maker Deluxe* (see Digital Resources). This can serve as a base for elaborated shared writing and will help with the transition from dependent writing to independent writing.

The *Sentence Maker Deluxe* has seven boxes of writing options. Students are initially asked to choose five of the boxes to complete when working independently. These include the *topic* and *because* statement boxes. The teacher can work with the class during shared writing to create pieces using all the sentence options and even add more as needed.

What to Write About

Overview

Students at all levels often express frustration over what to write about. If this problem is addressed, writing can move forward. When students are first learning to write, they are often assigned topics. As they progress, they are expected to take ownership of their topics. In this lesson, students learn strategies for using various picture and word cards to spark writing ideas.

Materials

- container labeled *Topics*
- picture/word flashcards; place in *Topics* container
- *Firefighter Word Card* (page 101); (see Digital Resources for a color version and for additional word cards)
- word books
- student copies of *Author Idea List* (page 102)

This lesson calls for picture/word flashcards and word books. The picture/word flashcards are level-appropriate cards with images and labels on them. Word books are books containing labeled pictures.

Procedure

1. Ask students to come to the carpet area and sit in view of the chart paper. Open a writing folder, and say, "Today, we are going to make an Author Idea List. Who am I talking about when I say Author Idea List?" Wait for answers. "That's right. If this is your folder, then I am talking about *you* being the author. This will be a list of ideas for you to write about!"

2. Say, "This chart is going to be my Author Idea List." Write *Author Idea List* at the top of the chart paper. Ask students, "What might you want to write about?" Give several students an opportunity to express their ideas, and write two of the ideas on the list. Draw a quick picture beside each idea. Tell students that one way for them to brainstorm ideas to write about is to use ideas from their own minds.

3. Next, pick up the *Topics* container, and say, "This label says *Topics*. A topic is an idea that you can write about. Inside the container, there are cards that have pictures and words on them. Let's find some topics to write about from this container."

- Call on a student volunteer to choose a card and share what is on the card with the class. Ask the student, "Can you think of something to write about a (name of the image on the card)?"

- After the student provides a detail about the topic, guide them to add further details, such as color, size, or actions. Write the word from the card on the chart, and draw a quick picture according to the details that the student has provided. Ask another student volunteer to choose a card, and repeat the same process.

4. Display the *Firefighter Word Card*, and show it to students. Say, "This is a word card. Word cards are usually all about one topic. This word card is all about firefighters. There are lots of words on it about firefighters."

- Read the words to students, and ask if anyone would like to write about something on the word card. Call on two students, and write the words for the ideas they choose on the chart. Say, "I think word cards are great for finding story topics."

What to Write About *(cont.)*

Procedure *(cont.)*

5. Pick up a book, and tell students, "This is a book. It has lots of words and pictures in it. Do you think there are lots of topics in this book you could write about? Let's find out!"

   • Open the book, and ask a student volunteer to tell you something they would want to write about on that page. Add that word to the chart with a quick picture. Repeat with a new page in the book, and add another word and picture to the chart.

6. Finally, refer to the sound chart. Say, "You aren't going to believe this, but there are 26 topics on our sound chart!" Call on two students to tell you topics they would want to write about from the chart, and add them and a drawing of each to the Author Idea List anchor chart.

7. Review the list with students. As they read the listed ideas, draw arrows and label where the ideas came from: *brain, topic basket, word cards, word book,* and *sound chart.* When the chart is finished, say, "This is a great list. It will always be on the wall to remind you where you can find ideas for writing. Now you know how to find ideas for your very own topic lists. Great job, authors!"

8. Following the lesson, distribute copies of *Author Idea List* to students, and have them put the lists in the fronts of their writing folders. Give students opportunities every few weeks to add ideas to their lists.

Cathy's Connections

If you prefer, get a clip art picture of a brain, take pictures of the *Topics* container, picture/word flashcards, *Firefighter Word Card,* books, and the sound chart to add to the *Author Idea List* anchor chart.

The chart can also be made into small student anchor charts for their writing folders. When students ask what they should write about, direct them to the class anchor chart and their own lists in their folders. The goal is for students to become responsible for their own topic selections and empowered to use the resources available to them.

Firefighter Word Card

fire station	fire truck	flames	fire extinguisher
walkie talkies	Dalmatian	flashlight	hose
nozzle	helmet	ax	fire hydrant
firefighter	ambulance	fire helicopter	ladder

Name _____

Author Idea List

Directions: List ideas you want to write about.

Squiggle Writing—Day 1

Overview

This lesson takes place over four days. Students are given a draw start or line squiggle and asked to create "the rest of the story" by completing the illustration. Then, students write about what they drew.

Materials

- drawing paper
- one or more mentor texts: *The Squiggle* by Carole Lexa Schaefer, *A Squiggly Story* by Andrew Larsen and Mike Lowery, *Not a Box* by Antoinette Portis, or *Not a Stick* by Antoinette Portis

Procedure

1. Seat students around a sheet of chart paper. Read a mentor text for squiggles if you have one. Introduce a "squiggle" by drawing one on chart paper. (Draw two lines intersecting to form a cross). Say, "Today, we are going to think about this squiggle and see if we can make something out of it."

2. Show students how you can make a window out of the cross you drew. Draw with a pencil, label the picture, then color it with a crayon.

3. Ask students if they have ideas about what they can make out of the same shape. As students tell you their ideas, sketch, color, and label the pictures.

4. Distribute drawing paper to students. Say, "Here is a paper for you to make your own cross-squiggle! You can choose one of our drawings on the chart to use, or you can make something new. Once you do that, label your picture." Give students time to draw, write, and color their squiggles.

5. When students are finished, call them back with their squiggles to share their ideas.

6. Complete the lesson by saying, "Today, we started our squiggle writing. You took a squiggle on the page and turned it into a fantastic and creative drawing. Tomorrow, we will do it with a new shape. I can't wait to see what you can create tomorrow!"

Squiggle Writing—Day 2

Materials
- drawing paper

Procedure

1. Gather students on the carpet, seated in view of a sheet of chart paper. Refer to the squiggle chart from Day 1, and say, "Yesterday, we had a squiggle with two lines that were crossed, and we made it into many things. Today, we are going to talk about how a shape can be turned in many directions."

2. Draw ten *V*s on a sheet of chart paper. Make the *V*s pointing up, down, left, and right. Make them big enough to be seen by the entire class. Say, "I have drawn several *V*s on this paper, but I have turned the *V* in many directions. What can we make using these *V*s today?" As students tell you their ideas, draw, color, and label the pictures.

3. When students have given many examples, send them to their seats with drawing paper. Tell students, "Today, it will be a little different because you can turn the paper in any direction you want to for your picture. Remember to draw, label, and color your picture."

4. Encourage students to draw something different from their neighbors. If you see too many bird beaks, rotate the page to a different angle and give students suggestions.

5. After students are finished, call them back to the carpet to share their illustrations. Say, "These are such great ideas. I can't wait to see what ideas you'll have tomorrow."

Cathy's Connections

It is important to introduce students to squiggle writing over several days and with multiple squiggles. Students need to get a complete understanding of what the activity is all about before they try it in a center.

The magic in this activity is creativity, and when students share their creativity with their classmates, it can inspire everyone to "think outside the box."

This is by far one of my favorite writing activities and centers of all time!

Squiggle Writing—Day 3

Materials

- drawing paper

Procedure

1. Gather students together on the carpet. Repeat the procedure from Day 2; however, today, use *U*-shaped squiggles drawn in various directions on the chart paper. Help students compose complete sentences for each of the squiggles. For example, "I see the rainbow."

2. Draw pictures of students' ideas, and label them with the sentence "I see the_____." This writing should be modeled and quickly written to illustrate to students how each picture will have a sentence.

3. Say, "Today, you will draw a *U*-shaped squiggle. You can turn the paper any way you want. After you draw your picture, you will write a sentence starting with "I see the_____."

4. Distribute drawing paper to students, and send them to their seats. Monitor students as they work on their drawings and sentences. Remind students to use capitals, spaces, and end marks as they write. Students may color their squiggle pictures after writing their sentences.

5. When students are finished, bring them back to the carpet to share their drawings and sentences. Say, "These are such creative ideas, and I love your sentences. You made sure to have your sentences start with capitals, use spaces, and remember end marks."

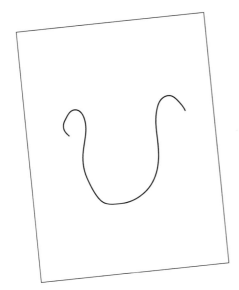

Squiggle Writing—Day 4

Materials
- drawing paper

Procedure

1. Begin the lesson with students at their desks. Distribute drawing paper to students.

2. Have students draw a zigzag line on their papers. Say, "Today, you are going to draw your own ideas on your zigzag squiggle papers. Don't forget, you can turn the paper any way you want. After you draw today, you will write a sentence using the sentence starter "Here is the ____." Write the sentence starter on the board, or show them the sentence phrases on the word wall to use as sentence starters.

3. Give students time to draw and write as you monitor and discuss their illustrations and sentences.

4. After students are finished, have them come to the carpet with their squiggle papers. Students will share their illustrations and their sentences. Say, "I am so impressed with your creations. I can't wait to see what you can do with squiggles in a center!"

Squiggle Writing—Day 4 *(cont.)*

Squiggle Writing Center

Students will continue Squiggle Writing in a center. This activity allows for student creativity, encourages students to stretch beyond "right and wrong," and motivates students to write. It can serve as an excellent informal assessment to document growth throughout the year.

Materials

- writing paper
- construction paper

Activities

Begin this center after teaching the Squiggle Writing lessons and after at least the first nine weeks of school to allow for instruction in sight words and sentence structure.

- Draw a different squiggle on nine sheets of paper to make masters. Then, copy the masters and collate them to make individual squiggle books for your students. When students come to this center, they choose a page, draw and color a picture using the squiggle, and then write about their squiggles. Tell students they have to choose a different squiggle from the other students at their table.

- For the first few weeks, students should write one sentence, but then the writing needs to be increased to at least two sentences, including a topic, color, size, or setting sentence from Sentence Maker (pages 89–98).

- For the third nine weeks, students are required to write four sentences about their squiggle using Sentence Maker.

- For the fourth nine weeks, encourage students to incorporate two different squiggles into one picture and write four to six sentences.

- Support students at this center by allowing them to dictate their sentences to an adult, or by providing students with sentence frames.

Opinion Writing—Day 1

Overview

This lesson takes place over five days and provides students with a strategy for writing an opinion paragraph. Both sides of an opinion are brainstormed, and students determine which side to write about. This strategy can be used by students during writing workshop and practiced at an independent writing center.

Materials

- chart paper

Procedure

1. Gather students on the carpet. Say, "This week, we will write about things we like. We could write about cake or cookies. Which do you like better? Turn to your neighbors, and tell them which dessert you like more: cake or cookies." Allow time for students to talk to their neighbors.

2. Continue by saying, "We could also write about whether chocolate or vanilla ice cream is better. Turn to your neighbors again, and tell them which ice cream you like more: chocolate or vanilla."

3. Allow time for conversation, and then tell students, "Let's write about which pets we like better: dogs or cats. Turn to your neighbors one more time, and tell them which pet you like more: dogs or cats."

4. When students are finished sharing with their neighbors, say, "We will need to decide which pet our class likes better: dogs or cats. We aren't going to decide right now, but we can write our title. Let's call our writing *Dogs or Cats?* Use Echo Writing (pages 18–19), Counting Words and Fold and Whisper (pages 52–53) to have students write the title on a sheet of chart paper. Draw students' attention to the question mark.

5. Complete the lesson by saying, "Today, we started our writing about which pet we like better: dogs or cats. I'm not sure which pet we will choose, but I am sure this is going to be great writing."

6. Save the chart with the title for Day 2.

Opinion Writing—Day 2

Materials

- writing chart (from Day 1)
- chart paper; draw two columns with the title *Dogs or Cats?*

Procedure

1. Seat students in front of the charts. Say, "Yesterday, we talked about how we might like one thing better than something else. We talked about cake or cookies. We talked about chocolate or vanilla ice cream. We also talked about dogs or cats. We even wrote a title for our writing about dogs or cats. Let's read the title together." Read the title with one-to-one matching and finger pointing. Ask students, "Why do we have a question mark at the end of the title?" (because we are asking a question)

2. Say, "Next, we are going to make a plan to write. We have this chart to help us (point to the two-column chart). We are only going to talk and write about dogs today. Let's think of three reasons we love dogs." Call on three students to give reasons for loving dogs. Use Echo Writing (pages 18–19) and Counting Words and Fold and Whisper (pages 52–53) as you write. Write abridged versions of three ideas students offer as bullet points. They will be made into complete sentences later in the week. It is important to show students how to make a prewrite list.

3. After recording three ideas, reread the list with students. Say, "I think dogs are fantastic. This is a great list of reasons why we love dogs. Tomorrow, we will write about why we love cats."

4. Save both charts for Day 3.

Dogs	or	Cats?
• lick us		
• cuddle with us		
• play fetch with us		

Opinion Writing—Day 3

Materials
- writing chart (from Days 1 and 2)
- Dogs or Cats? two-column chart (from Day 2)

Procedure

1. Seat students in full view of the two-column chart and the writing chart with the title *Dogs or Cats?* Say, "Yesterday, we made a list of some reasons why we love dogs. Let's reread the ideas." Lead students in rereading the dog side of the two-column chart.

2. Say, "Today, we get to make a list of all the great things we love about cats." Have students give reasons why they love cats. Write abridged versions of three ideas students offer as bullet points. They will be made into complete sentences later in the week. It is important to show students how to make a prewrite list.

Dogs	or	Cats?
• lick us		• sleep on our laps
• cuddle with us		• let us carry them
• play fetch with us		• sleep on our beds

3. Ask students to listen as you reread the list. Then say, "I like this list. I think cats are awesome. This is a great list of reasons why we love cats. Tomorrow, we are going to decide as a class if we like dogs or cats best."

4. Save both charts for Day 4.

Opinion Writing—Day 4

Materials

- writing chart (from Days 1–3)
- Dogs or Cats? two-column chart (from Days 2–3)
- *Dogs or Cats Ballots* (page 112; see Digital Resources for a color version or for ballots with additional topics); copy and cut out so there is one ballot for each student

Procedure

1. Begin the lesson with students at their desks with pencils available. Display the two-column chart and the writing chart. Say, "This week has been fun talking about dogs and cats and why we love them. Let's reread our lists." Lead students in rereading the lists. Then say, "Turn to your neighbors, and tell them if you like dogs or cats better."

2. Once students have had their discussions, distribute one *Dogs or Cats Ballot* to each student. Have students vote for their favorite pet by circling one of the pictures. After they have voted, tell them to put their ballot in a container and be seated on the carpet.

3. Count the ballots with students. Making a tally chart on the lists can add a math component to your lesson. After counting, declare a winner. Say, "Just like the election for our mayor or our president, when the votes are counted, there is a winner. Today's winner is _____. We will use the _____ side of our list on our prewrite to write about why we love _____."

4. Say, "Let's start by writing our main idea or topic sentence. We will use the title to help us." Reread the title, and ask students to count the words as you orally turn it into the main idea or topic sentence: *We like _____ better than _____*. Say, "How many words are in our sentence?" Use Echo Writing (pages 18–19) and Counting Words and Fold and Whisper (pages 52–53). Have students orally participate as you write the sentence.

5. When the topic sentence is finished, reread the first item on the corresponding prewrite list. Ask students to count the words as you turn the item into a complete sentence. Use Penmanship Oral Directions (pages 20–21) and Fold and Whisper as you write the first detail sentence.

6. Complete the lesson by saying, "Today, we started our writing about why we like _____ better. I'm so proud of the way you voted, accepted the results of our vote, and started writing our paper. I can't wait to finish this tomorrow."

7. Save both charts for Day 5.

Dogs or Cats?

1. lick us	1 sleep on our laps
2. cuddle with us	2. let us carry them
3 play fetch with us	3 sleep on our beds
11	9

Dogs or Cats Ballots

dogs

or

cats

dogs

or

cats

dogs

or

cats

dogs

or

cats

Opinion Writing—Day 5

Materials
- writing chart (from Days 1–4)
- Dogs or Cats? two-column chart (from Days 2–4)

Procedure

1. Seat students in front of the two-column chart and the writing chart. Say, "This has been a busy writing week. We had lots of great discussions, voted for dogs or cats, and started writing. Today, we are going to finish our writing." Reread what has been written so far.

2. Say, "Let's keep going." Continue turning two more ideas listed on the two-column chart into sentences, and write them as students orally participate using Echo Writing (pages 18–19) and Counting Words and Fold and Whisper (pages 52–53).

3. Say, "Finally, we need to write a closing sentence. It will summarize the whole story in one last sentence." Brainstorm ideas for sentences with students, and then say, "We had some great ideas. Let's write our closing sentence as *That's why we like _____ better than_____.*" Write the final sentence using the same strategies as for the previous sentences.

4. Reread the whole paragraph, and say, "This is a fantastic paper about why we love _____ . We have a super starting sentence, three great details, and a wonderful closing sentence. Great job!"

Note: A student template for the two-column chart called *This or That?* is on page 114.

> Dogs or Cats?
> We like dogs better than cats. Dogs like to lick us. Dogs cuddle with us. Dogs also play fetch with us. That's why we love dogs better than cats.

Cathy's Connections

Creating the two-column chart using student ideas and turning those ideas into sentences doesn't need to be a big lesson with kindergartners. Sometimes, an explanation is too big for a whole-group setting and can sideline the lesson. Giving a small explanation can be enough. I would simply tell students, "We are going to make a list, and instead of numbers, we will put a dot at the beginning of each item." Beginning on Day 4, when you are turning the title into a topic sentence and making sentences out of the bulleted comments, simply say, "Let's turn our ideas into sentences."

Name _____

This or That?

Directions: Draw what you like. List three reasons why.

_____   _____

_____   _____

_____   _____

_____   _____

_____   _____

Narrative Writing—Day 1

Overview

This lesson takes place over five days. Students learn a strategy for writing a narrative paragraph with at least three details. The cards used in this lesson can be moved into an independent writing center.

Materials

- *Going to the Zoo Narrative Writing Card* (left side of page 116; see Digital Resources for a color version and for additional topics)

Procedure

1. Seat students around a sheet of chart paper. Say, "This week, we will write about places we have been and what we did or saw there. This is called narrative writing, and it's a great way to connect with your reader."

2. Continue by showing students the *Going to the Zoo Narrative Writing Card.* Say, "We are going to write about our trip to the zoo. Turn and tell your neighbor something that you could see at the zoo." Allow time for conversation.

3. Point to the card, and say, "I saw a zookeeper, her keys, a big gate (oh, I wonder what was behind the gate), and an elephant. Today, we are only going to write the topic sentence and introduce the story to our reader. Let's make the opening sentence exciting. We could write something like *I want to tell you about my fantastic day at the zoo* or *You won't believe what I saw at the zoo!* Turn and talk to your partner about an exciting way to start the story."

4. Allow time for conversation, and ask three students for examples of an exciting opening sentence. Say, "Let's write *You won't believe what I saw at the zoo.* Let's count the words in our opening sentence." Repeat the sentence, and use your fingers to count the nine words in the sentence. Write the sentence on chart paper using Echo Writing (pages 18–19) and Counting Words and Fold and Whisper (pages 52–53).

5. When the sentence is finished, reread the whole sentence and remind students this is only the first sentence. Say, "Tomorrow, we will continue with our story about our trip to the zoo. Turn and talk to a partner, and tell how we can talk about the zookeeper in our story."

6. Save the writing chart for Day 2.

> The blank template on the right side of page 116 can be used for shared class experiences, such as field trips. Add a topic and details before sharing with students.

Going to the Zoo Narrative Writing Card

Going to the Zoo	Going to the _____
zookeeper	
keys	
gate	
elephant	

 124548—The Road to Independent Reading and Writing

Narrative Writing—Days 2–5

Materials

- writing chart (from Day 1)
- *Going to the Zoo Narrative Writing Card* (page 116; see Digital Resources for a color version)

Procedure

1. Gather students on the carpet, and review the *Going to the Zoo Narrative Writing Card* and the opening sentence composed yesterday.

2. Say, "Yesterday, we shared with the reader about our visit to the zoo, and we wrote a great introduction sentence. Today, we need to write about the zookeeper. Yesterday, I had you talk to your partner about the zookeeper. I heard lots of good talk." Call on three students to share their sentences about the zookeeper. After acknowledging students' responses, say "Let's write the sentence *The zookeeper let me help with her day.* Count the eight words, and use Echo Writing (pages 18–19) and Counting Words and Fold and Whisper (pages 52–53) to write the sentence.

3. After writing the sentence, say, "I love our sentence about the zookeeper. This is going to be a great story. Let's look at our *Going to the Zoo Narrative Writing Card* and see what we're going to write about tomorrow." Take time to look at the card and discuss what keys we could see at the zoo. Ask students to turn and talk about the keys to their carpet partners.

4. Continue adding to the story on Days 3–5, writing one sentence each day using the same methods and routines. Make sure to write a wrap-up sentence at the end of Day 5. Students should close with a simple *The trip was great.* or something similar.

Cathy's Connections

Sticky Note Narratives is one of my favorite spur of the moment writing techniques. Always have a stack of sticky notes near the classroom door. As students are entering the room, someone will inevitably come in with a tale to tell about the night before at home. "Mrs. Collier, my brother fell last night on his bike, and we had to go to the hospital. There was blood everywhere, and he had to get eight stitches." This is the perfect narrative for their journal. Take your sticky notes, and ask them to give you three words they need to write all about in their journal. For example, *hospital, blood, stitches.*

Narrative Writing—Days 2–5 (cont.)

Narrative Writing Center

Students will continue practicing narrative writing in a center. This activity allows for student creativity, encourages students to stretch beyond "right and wrong," and motivates students to write. It can serve as an excellent informal assessment to document growth throughout the year.

Materials

- writing paper
- *Narrative Writing Cards* (see Digital Resources); cut into two strips
- Narrative Writing Card blank template (page 116)

Activities

Introduce new *Narrative Writing Cards* in the center each week. Choose between removing previously used cards or leaving them in the center for students to use again as writing topics.

- Use the blank template to show a topic and details for shared class experiences, such as field trips.
- Build to having students create their own narrative writing cards using the template.
- Provide sentence starters to students who need additional support to complete this center independently.

Independent Journals

Overview

Students will write independently using picture prompts, writing pages, or independent prompts to describe topics or tell stories.

Materials

- student copies of *Journal Writing* (pages 120–121); may be assembled into booklets

Procedure

1. Distribute copies of *Journal Writing* or paper bound into a booklet to students. (This can be several sheets of paper inside a construction paper cover stapled in the middle.)

2. During a consistent time each day, have students take out their journals and work on writing independent stories. Students can begin new topics each day or continue writing about their previous topics.

3. Distribute copies of *Sentence Maker* (page 91) and *The Big 3* to students to use as reference when writing.

4. Remind students to use the classroom anchor charts.

5. Journals should be a place for daily writing practice. Although there is not a formal assessment, students can be held accountable with the Big 3, staying on topic, and providing details. Journals can be an excellent formative assessment to help direct whole-class teaching and to identify individual student needs.

Name _____

124548—The Road to Independent Reading and Writing   © Shell Education

Name

The Road to
Independent
Reading

Introduction to Reading

What do I know about teaching reading? I know so much more than when I started, but we're always learning more about better ways to serve our students, right?

When I started teaching, reading instruction was based on the words in the basal reading series. I had an "Aspects of Reading" class for elementary teachers in college, but that focused on the history of reading instruction and a few instructional strategies. As a teacher for students with disabilities, I used the basal and adapted it to my students, but that usually meant I just taught the same skills and sequence a little bit slower. Then, I got a copy of Merrill Linguistics to use with my students. I was so excited! Lessons were scaffolded and phonics based. My students made great progress, and they were excited to read.

I also think this is when my love of creating materials began. You see, I was only given books—no supporting materials or even Teacher Editions. I loved developing instructional materials to support my students. We started with *at* words and moved forward. Teaching reading with a concentration in phonics allowed students to understand and decode beautifully.

Fast forward five years, I had earned my master's degree in Early Education, and I left special education and my linguistic readers. The big swing to balanced literacy was in full motion. I was teaching "regular education" and knew I needed something to fill the gaps with my students who "just couldn't keep up." Balanced literacy seemed to be the answer. I learned about leveled texts, scaffolded lessons, and reading interventions based on oral reading records. I was in heaven. I loved being able to know where my students were in their reading journey and take them forward. In the same respect, students who were reading above level were able to continue to accelerate. I had a principal at the time who inspired me do more with reading, and I achieved my Advanced

Certificate in Reading.

Since that time, I have been relentless in finding what reading strategies work best for students. I have never been afraid of "new and improved," even when "new" didn't seem so new (you know in education, everything moves in a circle). I have been known to tell my teachers, we may have "tried that before," but we never tried it with these resources, at this time in educational research, and with these students.

Guess what? My linguistic readers from the '90s are back again, and it's a good thing. Teaching specific phonic skills for comprehension and decoding had a lot of merit then and has even more now. But, as a cautionary tale, I think we have to be very careful not to throw the baby out with the bathwater every time something is reinvented and understood. There must be a marriage of phonics and reading. The science of reading is definitely validating all that we knew about the value of phonics with undeniable clarity. I stood before my teachers two years ago, during year 30 of teaching, and told them we needed to shift our focus from multiple decoding cues to vowels. Vowels have all the power (more on that later). We're never too new or too experienced to learn more to help our students.

Phonological Awareness

According to the ILA Literacy Glossary, *phonological awareness* is the awareness of sounds of words in learning to read and spell. Phonological awareness does not involve letters—only sounds. It is a necessary building block of early literacy. Research shows that students who lack phonological awareness may eventually have difficulty understanding how to use and manipulate the letters for reading and spelling.

> There is considerable research showing how crucial developing phonological awareness is. It is estimated that 70–80% of students reading below grade level have phonological deficits.

The components of words can be distinguished in three ways: (1) by syllables, as */book/*, (2) by onsets and rimes, as */b/* and */ook/*, or (3) by phonemes, as */b/* and */oo/* and */k/*. Shown below are some activities that develop phonological awareness.

Phonological Awareness		
Syllables	**Intra-Syllable**	**Phonemic Awareness**
	Onset-Rime	
jump-ing—2 syllables	*j-ump-(ing)*	*/j/u/m/p/i/ng/*—6 phonemes
Syllables How many syllables are in this word?	**Onset-Rime Blending** Can you blend the onset and rime to tell the complete word?	**Phoneme Blending** Can you blend the sounds to make a word?
Syllable Blending Can you blend these sounds to make a word?	**Onset-Rime Segmentation** Can you break a word into onset and rime?	**Phoneme Segmentation** Can you separate the phonemes in a word?
Syllable Segmentation Can you break this word apart by sounds?		**Listening** Do these words sound the same?
Sentence Segmentation Can you tell me how many words are in the sentence?		**Alliteration** Do these words start with the same sound?
		Rhyming Do these words rhyme?

Phonological awareness activities can be done in whole group, small group, and individually. Students should not be seeing the written words during these activities. They will only be using oral language and pictures, if you have them available.

Nursery rhymes are an excellent resource for teaching phonological awareness. They have a rhythm and rhyme that give them a sing-song nature that make them fun to say over and over again. That also makes them easy to remember.

Provided in this section are examples of phonological awareness activities for three nursery rhymes: "Jack and Jill," "Itsy Bitsy Spider," and "Humpty Dumpty." Activities described in the chart above and within the lessons serve as an example of ways to expand students' phonological awareness and can be used with any nursery rhyme. Following the lesson plans are charts for these nursery rhymes with suggested questions to ask and words to use from the nursery rhymes.

Syllable Awareness

Overview

Students will learn the words to the nursery rhyme "Jack and Jill" until they can say it independently. Then, use words from the poem to practice syllable phonological awareness activities.

Materials

- "Jack and Jill" nursery rhyme

Procedure

1. Orally present the words from the poem. Ask students to determine the syllables in each word. Students can count the syllables in a variety of ways, but having students count together is a necessity. Teach students to *golf clap count* the syllables at the same time. This is a modified golf clap technique. As they clap the syllables, teach them to clap with one finger, then two fingers, and so on. While using the counting clap, students can quickly identify the number of syllables in a word. Suggested words to use from the nursery rhyme: *Jack, Jill, hill, fetch, pail, water, fell, broke, tumbling, after.*

2. Present syllables of words with an exaggerated pause in between the syllables (*/wa/* pause */ter/*). Have students blend the syllables together to say the word normally (*water*). Suggested words to use: *wa-ter, tum-bl-ing, af-ter, bro-ther, sis-ter, hill-side, buck-et.*

Jack and Jill

Jack and Jill went up the hill,

To fetch a pail of water.

Jack fell down and broke his crown,

And Jill came tumbling after.

3. Present multisyllabic words to students, and ask them to break the words into syllables. They will exaggerate the break between syllables. This is the reverse of the previous activity. As students are accomplishing breaking the word into syllables, ask them to isolate certain syllables. For example, the first syllable in the word *bucket* is *buck*. They can practice counting syllables by using the modified golf clap and count method. This should help students isolate specific syllables. Suggested words to use: *water, tumbling, after, brother, sister, hillside, bucket.*

Cathy's Connections

Students often have a difficult time separating words into syllables. One technique to help them feel the syllables is to have them hold the palms of their hands under their chins while saying the word. Each time their chins drop and hit their hands is a part of a word or a syllable. Try it!

Phonological Awareness Skills Suggestions
Jack and Jill

Skill	Question	Suggested Words/Sentences
Syllables	How many syllables are in this word?	**1-syllable words:** *Jack, Jill, hill, ran, fetch* **2-syllable word:** *water* **3-syllable word**: *tumbling*
Syllable Blending	Can you blend these sounds to make a word?	*wa-ter, af-ter*
Syllable Segmentation	Can you break this word apart by sounds?	*water, after*
Sentence Segmentation	Can you tell me how many words are in a sentence?	Jack ran up the hill. Jill did, too. He wanted water. Jack fell down. Jill fell down, too.
Onset and Rime Blending	Can you blend the onset and rime to tell the complete word?	*J-ack, J-ill, r-an* **Additional Words:** *r-an; c-an, m-an* *h-ill, b-ill, f-ill* *cr-own; d-own, g-own*
Onset and Rime Segmentation	Can you break a word into onset and rime?	*pail, fell, down*
Phoneme Blending	Can you blend the sounds to make a word?	**2-phoneme words**: /u/p/, /t/oo/ **3-phoneme words:** /j/a/ck/, /p/ai/l/ **4-phoneme words:** /f/e/t/ch/, /w/a/t/er/
Phoneme Segmentation	Can you separate the phonemes in a word?	*up, to, Jack, Jill, pail, fetch, went, water*
Listening/Discerning Sounds in Words	Do these words sound the same?	*Jack/Jack; hill/home; Jill/hill; water/water; hill/bell; fetch/farm*
Alliteration	Do these words start the same?	Jill likes to juggle jelly beans. Jack jumps over a juice box. Put pizza in the pail.
Rhyming	Do these two words rhyme?	*Jack/back; Jill/fill; pail/hill; water/daughter*
	Can you think of words that rhyme?	*hill—fill, bill* *pail—whale, sail, nail* *went—sent, bent, lent* *fell—bell, sell, tell*

Intra-Syllable Awareness

Overview

Students will learn the words to the nursery rhyme "Itsy Bitsy Spider" until they can say it independently. Then, use words from the poem to practice intra-syllable phonological awareness activities.

Materials

- "Itsy Bitsy Spider" nursery rhyme

Procedure

1. Make up sentences related to the topic of the nursery rhyme. For example, *The spider fell down.* Have students stand and march in place, stomping one foot per word as they say the sentence. Then, have them golf-clap count (page 126) the sentence to determine the number of words in the sentence. They can hold their fingers up to show the correct number of words. Suggested sentences: *The itsy bitsy spider went up the water spout. The rain started to fall. The spider fell down. The spider went back up the water spout.*

2. Segment words from the nursery rhyme into onsets and rimes. (**Reminder:** The onset is the letter or letters before the first vowel. The rime is the vowel and the letters after the vowel.) Have students blend the onset and rime together to say the whole word. For example, say, "Blend together /w/ pause /ent/." Students should respond with the word *went.* Suggested words: w-ent, sp-out, r-ain, c-ame, s-un, l-and.

3. Provide students with the word, and have them provide the onset and rime. This is a reverse of the previous activity. For example, say, "The word is *rain.*" Students should say: /r/ pause /ain/. Suggested words: *w-ent, sp-out, r-ain, c-ame, s-un, l-and.* Extend the activity by having students name other words that have the same rime. For example, for the word *land,* students could say: *sand, band,* and *hand.*

Itsy Bitsy Spider

The itsy bitsy spider went up the water spout.

Down came the rain and washed the spider out.

Out came the sun and dried up all the rain,

And the itsy bitsy spider went up the spout again.

Phonological Awareness Skills Suggestions
Itsy Bitsy Spider

Skill	Question	Suggested Words/Sentences
Syllables	How many syllables are in this word?	**1-syllable words:** *went, up, down, came, rain* **2-syllable words:** *itsy, bitsy, spider, water, again*
Syllable Blending	Can you blend these syllables to make a word?	*it-sy, bit-sy, wa-ter, spi-der, a-gain*
Syllable Segmentation	Can you break this word apart by sounds?	*itsy, bitsy, water, spider, again*
Sentence Segmentation	Can you tell me how many words are in a sentence?	The itsy bitsy spider went up the water spout. The rain started to fall. The spider fell down. The spider went back up the water spout.
Onset and Rime Blending	Can you blend the onset and rime to tell the complete word?	*w-ent, sp-out, r-ain, c-ame, s-un, l-and*
Onset and Rime Segmentation	Can you break a word into onset and rime?	*went, spout, rain, came, sun, land*
Phoneme Blending	Can you blend the sounds to make a word?	**2-phoneme words:** /u/p/ **3-phoneme words:** /r/ai/n/, /c/a/m/, /a/n/d/ **4-phoneme words:** /l/a/n/d/, /w/e/n/t/, /w/o/t/r/ **5-phoneme words:** /s/p/i/d/r/
Phoneme Segmentation	Can you separate the phonemes in a word?	*up, rain, came, and, land, went, water, spider*
Listening/Discerning Sounds in Words	Do these words sound the same?	*spider/spider; went/water; land/like; down/down; came/cat*
Alliteration	Do these words start the same?	The spider spills the spaghetti. The rain ran into the river.
Rhyming	Do these two words rhyme?	*went/sent; land/band; sun/run; rain/pain*
	Can you think of words that rhyme?	*went—sent, tent, spent, lent* *land—sand, band, hand* *sun—run, bun, fun* *main—pain, gain, rain*

Phonemic Awareness

Overview

Students will learn the words to the nursery rhyme "Humpty Dumpty" until they can say it independently. Then, use words from the poem to practice phonemic phonological awareness activities.

Materials

- "Humpty Dumpty" nursery rhyme

Procedure

1. Choose a word from the poem. Offer a second word to students. Sometimes the two words should rhyme, and sometimes they should not rhyme. Ask students to show you thumbs up if the two words rhyme and thumbs down if the two words do not rhyme. For example, say, "Do *king/ring* rhyme?" Students should show thumbs up. Say, "Do *men/call* rhyme?" Students should show thumbs down. When two words rhyme, encourage students to think of additional words that rhyme. For the words *king/ring*, students could also offer up *sing*, *bring*, and *wing*. Suggested words: *king/ring, men/pen, wall/fall, sat/wall, great/mat, again/had.*

2. Segment the sounds of a word from the nursery rhyme. Have students blend the sounds together. For example, say, "Blend together these sounds, /m/ pause /e/ pause /n/." Students should respond with the word *men*. Suggested words: *sat, wall, fall, great, horses, king.*

3. Provide students with a word from the nursery rhyme, and have them segment the word. This is a reversal of roles from the previous activity. For example, provide students with the word *king*. Students should respond by segmenting the sounds: /k/ pause /i/ pause /n/ pause /g/. Suggested words: *on, fall, men, great, again.*

Humpty Dumpty

Humpty Dumpty sat on a wall.

Humpty Dumpty had a great fall.

All the king's horses and all the king's men

Couldn't put Humpty together again.

Phonological Awareness Skills Suggestions
Humpty Dumpty

Skill	Question	Suggested Words/Sentences
Syllables	How many syllables are in this word?	**1-syllable words:** *sat, wall, had, great, fall, men* **2-syllable words:** *humpty, dumpty, horses, again* **3-syllable words:** *together*
Syllable Blending	Can you blend these sounds to make a word?	*hump-ty, dump-ty, hor-ses, a-gain, to-geth-er*
Syllable Segmentation	Can you break this word apart by sounds?	*humpty, dumpty, horses, again, together*
Sentence Segmentation	Can you tell me how many words are in a sentence?	Humpty Dumpty sat on a wall. Humpty Dumpty had a great fall. No one could help Humpty Dumpty.
Onset and Rime Blending	Can you blend the onset and rime to tell the complete word?	*s-at, w-all, k-ing, m-en* **Additional Words:** *s-at, f-at, c-at* *w-all, t-all, h-all* *k-ing, s-ing, th-ing*
Onset and Rime Segmentation	Can you break a word into onset and rime?	*sat, wall, king, men*
Phoneme Blending	Can you blend the sounds to make a word?	**2-phoneme words:** /o/n/ **3-phoneme words:** /f/o/l/, /m/e/n/ **4-phoneme words:** /g/r/a/t/, /a/g/e/n/
Phoneme Segmentation	Can you separate the phonemes in a word?	*on, fall, men, great, again*
Listening/Discerning Sounds in Words	Do these words sound the same?	*Humpty/Dumpty; great/great; wall/fell; horse/hand*
Alliteration	Do these words start the same?	The horse had a hair. The king came to the court with a kite. The fan fell on my foot.
Rhyming	Do these two words rhyme?	*king/ring; men/pen, wall/fall; sat/fat*
	Can you think of words that rhyme?	*king—ring, sing* *men—pen, when* *wall—fall, call* *sat—fat, cat*

Phonics

Phonics is the simple task of matching the letter to the sound. However, this isn't always a simple task. Students should be directed in letter/sound matching activities from the beginning of their reading journey. The journey with phonics starts from the first day, drawing students' attention to the sounds in words and discussing the letters that match the sounds.

One very important task is making sure students understand the difference between consonants and vowels. Recognizing and sorting them early will set in motion the understanding of the importance of vowels. Coloring, circling, and otherwise distinguishing consonants from vowels helps students understand the importance of both when word building.

In the past few years, I have shifted my thinking about the value of vowels. Not that I haven't tried to express the importance of vowels, I have always taught my students to understand that vowels are tricky. I would say, "Go slowly and think carefully about the sound of the vowel." I have taught them to try decoding a word with the short vowel first, then trying it with a long vowel sound. But recently, I have come to understand the distinction between the importance and the value when talking about vowels. Vowels control the world. Maybe that's a bit dramatic, but they control a lot in a word. They tend to be the part of the word where the sounds have the most opportunity for changing. We need to teach students to think about the vowels and what they *could be* doing in a word. We need to teach them "Good Options." Good Options are based on the probability of how the vowel will work.

I teach students phonics patterns based on the following continuum:

1. Initial Consonants
2. Ending Consonants
3. Short Vowels
4. Beginning Blends with Short Vowel Words
5. Digraphs with Short Vowel Words
6. Ending Blends with Short Vowel Words
7. Long Vowel Patterns
8. Absolutes

I use anchor charts to help introduce each phonics pattern. Having the anchor charts available for students to reference helps create a classroom of learners who have the resources to become independent.

Many of the lessons described in this section can be repeated with any of the phonics patterns on the continuum.

Beginning Sounds

Overview

The sound chart serves as a starting point for phonics. Students can easily make connections with beginning sounds and the pictures on the chart. The pictures help everyone in the class have the same reference point.

Materials

- student copies of *Sound Chart* (page 17)
- *Sound Picture Cards* (pages 134–137); cut apart

Procedure

1. Have students take out their copies of *Sound Chart*, or distribute copies to students as needed.

2. Display individual picture cards. Have students place a counter on their sound charts on the picture that has the same initial sound. For example, hold up a picture of a *bird*, and ask students, "Which picture on our sound chart starts the same as *b-b-b-bird*?"

3. Have students touch the corresponding square on their sound charts using their index fingers. Tell students to shout out the picture name on the sound chart. Review both words as you emphasize the initial sound. Say, "Yes, *b-b-b-bird* and *b-b-b-bear* both start with /b/."

4. Repeat the routine for approximately 5–7 minutes. Repeat this lesson multiple days until students become skilled. Practice in small groups or one-to-one with students needing additional support or practice in small groups.

5. Extend the activity by asking students to name the picture and the letter, establishing a sound/symbol correspondence.

> For added support, you may want to give options. "Which picture on our sound chart starts the same as *b-b-b bird?* Does it start the same as *g-g-g gate* or *b-b-b bear?*"

Sound Picture Cards

Sound Picture Cards *(cont.)*

Sound Picture Cards *(cont.)*

124548—The Road to Independent Reading and Writing

Sound Picture Cards *(cont.)*

Ending Sounds

Overview

Once students can easily identify beginning sounds, ending sounds are the next easiest sounds in words to hear. It is easy to elongate and emphasize most ending sounds in words. In this lesson, students identify ending sounds in words and write the corresponding letters.

Materials

- *Sound Picture Cards* (pages 134–137)
- student whiteboards and whiteboard markers

Procedure

1. Gather students on the carpet. Ensure each student has a whiteboard and marker.

2. Display a picture card. Say the word for students. Have them repeat the word.

3. Ask students to identify the sound heard at the end of the word. For example, hold up a picture of *gum*, and ask students, "Which sound do you hear at the end of the word *gum-m-m*?" Remind students to refer to the sound chart for support in identifying sounds or the corresponding letters.

4. Have students write the corresponding letter on their whiteboards.

5. Repeat the routine for approximately 5–7 minutes. Repeat this lesson multiple days until students become skilled at identifying ending sounds and writing their corresponding letters. Practice with students needing additional support or practice in small groups.

Next Steps

Display a set of three picture cards. Ensure that two of the pictures have the same ending sounds. Have students identify which pair of words have the same ending sounds. Repeat with other sets of cards. Build to having students choose from five picture cards.

Cathy's Connections

When introducing ending sounds, I initially stay away from ending blends and digraphs, as they complicate the early stages. That being said, the final /k/ sound is complicated. The /k/ ending can be represented with *c, k,* or *ck*. Determining the ending spelling depends on the vowel. Use *k* when following a long vowel or vowel team as in *book* and *ck* when following a short vowel. The final *c* is written when it's a multisyllabic word with a short vowel in the final syllable as in *topic*.

Short Vowels

Overview

Students learn a song to help them remember the vowels, and a routine for practicing reading rimes and corresponding words is introduced. Students will practice reading lists of rimes and words for a particular short vowel.

Materials

- *Vowel Charts* (see Digital Resources); display on wall
- *Short Vowel Rime Charts* (pages 141–143); copy on cardstock, cut charts apart, collate together, punch a hole in the corner, and place on a binder ring (1 per student); enlarge a copy to 200% for modeling
- binder rings (1 per student)

Procedure

1. Gather students on the carpet. Say, "Today, we are going to learn about special letters called *vowels*. These letters are like glue that hold words together. The vowels are *a, e, i, o,* and *u*." Point to the Vowel Charts on the wall, and remind students that those charts are in yellow because when we see them, we have to slow down and play close attention.

2. Teach students the words to "The Vowel Song" by singing a line and then having students echo. Continue this method until you have sung the entire song. You may choose to write the words to the song on a sheet of chart paper, so you can point to the words as you sing. This will help emphasize concepts of print, such as reading left to right, top to bottom, as well as one-to-one correspondence. Sing the song several times once students know the words.

3. Distribute the *Short Vowel Rime Chart* rings to students. Allow them to flip through the charts to see what is on the ring. Explain that the class will focus on practicing one vowel at a time.

4. Have students turn to the short *a* chart. Practice reading the words on the chart. For example: *ab, cab; ad, sad; ag, bag,* and so on.

5. Practice reading the short *a* chart each day until students are proficient. Then, move on to another vowel. Remember to go back and practice reading previously mastered charts as you proceed through the ring. After vowels are taught in isolation, teaching them in comparison to one another is important. The sounds for short *e* and short *i* are very similar and difficult for students to discern. Students will need ample exposure to these two vowels before comparing words with the two vowels.

Cathy's Connections

Vowels are the trickiest part of any phonics lessons. Highlighting vowels with yellow on the classroom sound chart and on students' individual *Sound Charts* (page 17) helps students identify them. Strategies such as Stoplight Writing (pages 37–41) can help students practice matching letters to sounds with vowels. I have always taught vowels as the glue and the part of the word that makes us pause and stretch the word carefully. But in fact, vowels are the key to reading, spelling, and writing. When students understand vowels, they can decode, and possibly encode, more easily.

The Vowel Song

(sung to the tune of "The Farmer in the Dell")

Words need a vowel.
Words need a vowel.
Consonants can't do it all,
Words need a vowel.

The vowel is the glue.
The vowel is the glue.
Words can fall apart real quick,
But the vowel is the glue.

A, e, i, o, u
A, e, i, o, u
Sometimes y, and we know why,
The vowels are the glue.

Short Vowel Rime Charts

Short *a*		Short *e*	
ă 🍎		ě	
ab – cab	an – fan	eb – web	en – pen
ack – back	ap – cap	ed – sled	ep – step
ad – sad	ash – crash	eg – beg	est – vest
ag – bag	at – hat	ell – well	et – net
am – ham	ax – wax	em – hem	

124548—The Road to Independent Reading and Writing

Short Vowel Rime Charts *(cont.)*

Short *i*		Short *o*	
Ĭ		Ŏ	
ib – bib	ill – hill	ob – cob	on
ick – sick	im – him	ock – lock	op – top
id – lid	in – bin	od – rod	ot – cot
iff – sniff	ip – dip	off	ox – box
ig – big	it – hit	og – dog	

Short Vowel Rime Charts *(cont.)*

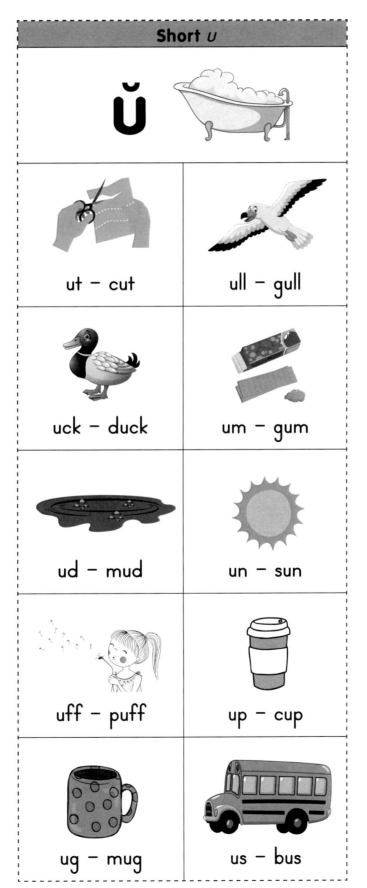

Short *u*	
Ŭ	
ut – cut	ull – gull
uck – duck	um – gum
ud – mud	un – sun
uff – puff	up – cup
ug – mug	us – bus

Short Vowel Rimes

Overview

Introducing rimes to students is an excellent way for them to begin to see patterns in words. In this lesson, students identify words with the same rime, and then use the rimes they know to spell new words.

Materials

- *Short Vowel Rime Chart* for short *a* (page 141)
- student copies of *Short Vowel a Rime Match* (page 145); enlarge to 200% for modeling

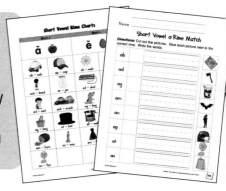

Procedure

1. Gather students on the carpet. Have students chant-read the rimes and corresponding words on their *Short Vowel Rime Chart* for short *a*.

2. Display the enlarged *Short Vowel a Rime Match*. Guide students to recognize that the rimes on this chart are the same as on the chart they practice reading each day.

3. Say, "There are many more words for each of these rimes than the ones we have been reading." Ask students to name some other words that have the *ab* rime (e.g., *dab, gab, jab, lab, nab, tab, crab, stab*).

4. Display the *tab* picture card. Say the word *tab*, emphasizing the *ab* rime. Model how to glue the picture of the *tab* next to the *ab* rime. Tell students, "Since these words have the same ending sounds, it makes it easy for us to spell the word *tab*. I hear /t/, so I will write *t*. Then I hear /ab/, so I will write *a-b*." Write the word *tab* in the box next to the picture.

5. Repeat the process with the remaining pictures.

6. Provide students with their own copies of *Short Vowel a Rime Match*. Have them complete the activity by matching the pictures to their correct rimes and spelling the words.

Have students complete each Short Vowel Rime Match sheet (pages 145–149) as you introduce each short vowel rime or as students are ready for it. Consider stapling all the pages together into a little book so students have a personal resource to reference as they write.

Name _____

Short Vowel *a* Rime Match

Directions: Cut out the pictures. Glue each picture next to the correct rime. Write the words.

ab		
ad		
ag		
am		
an		
ap		
at		
ax		

Name _____

Short Vowel e Rime Match

Directions: Cut out the pictures. Glue each picture next to the correct rime. Write the words.

eb		
ed		
eg		
em		
en		
et		

124548—The Road to Independent Reading and Writing

© Shell Education

Short Vowel *i* Rime Match

Directions: Cut out the pictures. Glue each picture next to the correct rime. Write the words.

ib		_____
id		_____
ig		_____
in		_____
ip		_____
it		_____
ix		_____

Short Vowel o Rime Match

Directions: Cut out the pictures. Glue each picture next to the correct rime. Write the words.

ob		
od		
og		
op		
ot		
ox		

Name _____

Short Vowel *u* Rime Match

Directions: Cut out the pictures. Glue each picture next to the correct rime. Write the words.

ub		
ud		
ug		
um		
un		
up		
us		
ut		

Beginning Blends

Overview

In this lesson, students learn about what blends are and then practice hearing them as they use the beginning sounds of words to write new words. Of course, the beginning sound of the new word has a blend, too!

Materials

- *Beginning Blends Poster* (page 151; see Digital Resources for a color version)
- *Beginning Blends Sound Chart* (page 152; see Digital Resources for a color version)
- whiteboards and markers; one per student
- student copies of *Beginning Blends Practice* (pages 153–154)
- *Beginning Blends Pictures* (page 155); cut in strips (one per student)

Procedure

1. Gather students on the carpet. Display the *Beginning Blends Poster*. Say, "Some words have two sounds at the beginning that go together. Each letter keeps its own sound, but instead of separating the sounds, we blend the two sounds together. We call these sounds *blends*.

2. Display the *Beginning Blends Sound Chart*. Tell students that this is another sound chart they can learn more about and use. Guide students through a routine for chanting the *Beginning Blends Sound Chart* (see Sound Chart, page 17). Chant this chart for several days until students are comfortable with beginning blends before proceeding to the next activity.

3. Tell students, "Today, we are going to practice listening for some of the blends we have been chanting. When we hear blends, we need to remember to write the letters for both of the sounds that go together to make the blend."

4. Say, "I'm going to say some blends. You write the letters for the two sounds you hear in the word." Name the following words for students, one at a time: *frog, glue, dragon, plan, brush, slide,* and *skunk*. Have students record the blend at the beginning of each word on their whiteboards and show them to you before going on to the next word. Segment the word more slowly, so students can hear each sound of the blend if needed.

5. Distribute *Beginning Blends Practice* and a strip of *Beginning Blends Pictures* to each student. Have students write the initial sound of each picture, including the beginning blend of the first picture. Students should then circle the blend and glue the corresponding picture.

When first introduced, blends should be used to decode short vowel words, such as *club, slam,* and *twig*. More complicated blends can be used with long vowel patterns, such as *braid, space,* and *twine*. Encoding and decoding are important skills that students must practice regularly.

Beginning Blends

two consonants that go together,
but keep their own sound

bl–   fl–
br–   fr–
cl–   gl–
cr–   gr–
dr–   pl–

pr–   sn–
sc–   sp–
sk–   st–
sl–   tr–
sm– tw–

Beginning Blends Sound Chart

bl blocks	br brush	cl clam	cr crab	dr drill
fl flower	fr frog	gl glue	gr grill	pl plug
pr present	sc scale	sk skull	sl sleep	sm smile
sn snail	sp spoon	st stamp	sw swing	tr trash
tw twig				

Beginning Blends Practice

Directions: Write the beginning sound for each picture. Circle the blend. Glue the correct picture.

1.

2.

3.

4.

5.

Beginning Blends Practice

Directions: Write the beginning sound for each picture. Circle the blend. Glue the correct picture.

1.

2.

3.

4.

5.

Beginning Blends Pictures

Teacher: Give this set of pictures to students to use to complete page 153.

Teacher: Give this set of pictures to students to use to complete page 154.

Digraphs

Overview

Digraphs are two letters that give us one new sound. We can't distinguish the individual letters because a new sound is created. In this lesson, students learn about digraphs and sort words by digraphs.

Materials

- *Digraphs Poster* (page 157; see Digital Resources for a color version)
- *Beginning Digraphs Sound Chart* (page 158); cut apart
- *Beginning Digraph Pictures* (pages 159–160); cut apart

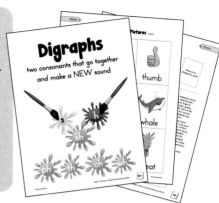

Procedure

1. Write the word *plant* on the board. Underline the blend *pl*. Remind students that in words with beginning blends, both sounds in the blend can be heard. Emphasize both the /p/ and /l/ sounds in the word *plant*.

2. Say the word *shell*. Have students isolate the initial sound in the word *shell* (/sh/). Explain to students that this is a sound that is not on the Sound Wall. Write the word *shell* on the board. Say, "I'm going to pronounce this word giving each letter its typical sound." Pronounce shell /s/h/e/ll. Tell students, "That doesn't sound right." Underline the *sh* in the word. Tell students these letters work together to make the /sh/ sound.

3. Display the *Digraphs Poster*. Tell students that some sounds are written by putting two consonants together to make a new sound. Point out the two consonants for each digraph, and emphasize the new sound.

4. Display the cards created by cutting apart the *Beginning Digraphs Sound Chart* and placing them in a pocket chart or taping them to the board.

5. Tell students they are going to help sort some pictures with digraphs. Display the *Beginning Digraph Pictures*, one picture at a time. Have students identify the digraph sound heard at the beginning of the word. Work with students to place the picture under the correct digraph header. Continue sorting the remaining pictures.

6. Review the pictures under each digraph header to emphasize the many words with the same beginning digraph.

7. Repeat this activity as needed. Or place the pieces in a center, and have students sort the pictures independently. Place the *Digraphs Poster* on the Sound Wall for students to reference.

See the Digital Resources for *Ending Digraphs Sound Chart* and *Ending Digraph Pictures*. The same activity can be repeated with ending digraphs.

Digraphs

two consonants that go together and make a NEW sound

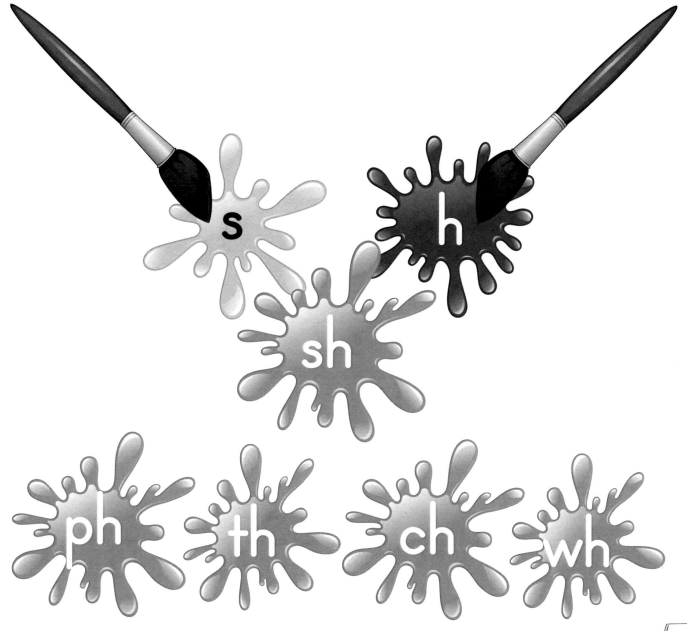

Beginning Digraphs Sound Chart

ch

chick

sh

shell

th

thorn

wh

whisk

Beginning Digraphs Pictures

chair

chop

cheese

check

chip

sheep

shark

shoe

shovel

Beginning Digraphs Pictures (cont.)

ship	three	thumb
thread	thermos	whale
whistle	wheel	wheat

Ending Blends

Overview

This lesson builds on the Beginning Blends lesson (pages 150–155) by introducing students to ending blends. Students listen to words and record the sounds they hear in the words. They use crayons to circle the letters that form the ending blends.

Materials

- *Ending Blends Sound Chart* (page 162; see Digital Resources for a color version)
- student copies of *Writing Words with Blends* (page 164)
- *Ending Blends Picture Cards* (page 163); cut apart

Procedure

1. Display the *Ending Blends Sound Chart*. Remind students of the beginning blends they learned about previously. Say, "Two consonants can be together at the end of a word, too. Today, we are going to practice listening for the sounds in the words, including the consonant ending blends.

2. Guide students through a routine for chanting the *Ending Blends Sound Chart*. Chant this chart for several days until students are comfortable with ending blends before proceeding to the next activity.

3. Distribute copies of *Writing Words with Blends* to students. Display one of the *Ending Blends Picture Cards*. Say the word aloud to students, and have them repeat it.

4. Teach students to tap the individual sounds in the words into their hands. Hold the palm of one hand out in front. Tap one finger at a time onto the hand with the palm, putting out a new finger for each sound. (Each of the words on the picture cards has four sounds; however, this routine will help students hear the segmented sounds in the word.)

5. Have students write the letters that match each of the four sounds they hear in the word in the boxes on their activity sheets. Confirm the spelling by having the class chant it aloud. Have students revise their spellings if needed. Work together as a class to determine the two consonants that form the ending blend. Have students use red crayons to draw circles around those boxes. Then, have students draw pictures of the word they wrote.

6. Continue the routine with other picture cards.

Cathy's Connections

Blends keep their own sounds, so anchor charts with a "blender" don't really represent what a blend is. If I put ingredients in a blender and push a button, the foods don't always retain their taste, so I'm hesitant to use a blender to represent blends. Instead, on the anchor chart for blends, I use peanut butter and jelly. They go together but don't lose their own taste.

Ending Blends Sound Chart

ct act	ft left	mb thumb
mp stamp	nd land	ng king
nk pink	nt plant	pt swept
sk mask	sp wasp	st forest

124548—The Road to Independent Reading and Writing

Ending Blends Picture Cards

Writing Words with Blends

Directions: Listen to each word. Write each sound you hear.
Draw a picture of the word.

1.

2.

3.

4.

5.

6.

Long Vowel Patterns

Overview

This lesson serves as an introduction to long vowel spelling patterns. Students learn several ways to spell the long *a* sound, including one that is very OMG (Oh My Goodness)!

Materials

- *Long Vowel Rime Card—long a* (page 166; see Digital Resources for a color version)
- *Long a Picture Cards* pages 167–170; see Digital Resources for color versions)

Procedure

1. Place the *Long Vowel Rime Card—long a* on the wall or easel. Ask students to come sit in view of the wall or easel. Say, "Today, we are going to talk about long vowel *a* sounds. Long vowels are vowels that say their names."

2. Point to the *Long Vowel Rime Card—long a*. Say, "The one thing that makes long vowels a little complicated is there are different spelling patterns. We're going to look at those patterns today."

3. Point to the cake and the corresponding spelling pattern. Tell students that this is a common spelling pattern to have a vowel, then a consonant, and then an *e* at the end of the word. Explain that the *e* at the end is silent in this spelling pattern. Say, "Some people call this *e* a bossy *e* or a magic *e* because the *e* has power. We're going to say, 'the *e* makes the *a* say *a*.' So if we look at this card, the *e* is making the *a* say *a*, so it doesn't say căk, it makes it say *caaaake*." (Stretch the long *a* sound and show the corresponding picture card for the pattern.)

4. Say, "Now, let's listen to some more long *a* words with a different spelling pattern. This pattern is *ai*, and it is a spelling pattern for long *a* that is found in the middle of a word. Let's look at the word *train* and find the *ai* pattern." Once students identify the pattern, show them the picture cards with the *ai* pattern. Make sure they identify the spelling as *ai*.

5. Explain the *ay* spelling pattern to students. Explain to students that *ay* is typically at the end of the word, such as in *play*, although the word *crayon* is an exception to this. However, this exception is based on two syllables. Display and discuss the picture cards for the *ay* spelling pattern.

6. Add the last long *a* vowel pattern. This is the "Oh My Goodness" long *a* sound. Say, "The last long *a* pattern looks like this." Point to the picture of *weigh*. Say, "Oh My Goodness, that says the long *a* sound, but there's no *a*. The *e-i-g-h* when we put them together makes the long *a* sound. Oh My Goodness." Have students make the long *a* sound. Share the other picture cards that have the *eigh* long *a* pattern.

7. Once all the long *a* patterns are added to the wall, review them. Say, "Now, we have learned all about long *a* patterns. We saw three ways to spell the long *a* pattern and one Oh My Goodness way. Who can remember the long *a* patterns with an *a*?" Wait for answers. "Who can tell me the Oh My Goodness pattern for long *a*?" Wait for answers. "Pat yourself on the back. I'm so proud of you."

> **Repeat this lesson with the other vowel patterns as students are ready. See the Digital Resources for cards for the other vowels.**

Long Vowel Rime Card—long *a*

a–e	cake	
ai	train	
ay	play	
eigh	weigh	

Long *a* Picture Cards

game

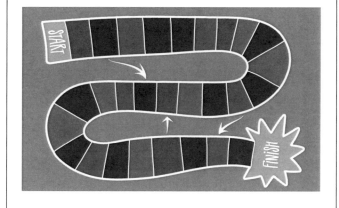

vase

grape

skate

Long *a* Picture Cards *(cont.)*

pail

snail

chain

drain

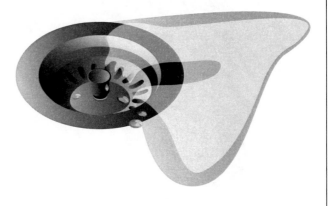

Long *a* Picture Cards *(cont.)*

hay

gray

jay

spray

Long *a* Picture Cards *(cont.)*

weigh

sleigh

eight

eighty

Long Vowels

Overview

A routine for practicing reading rimes and corresponding words is reinforced. Students practice reading lists of rimes and words for a particular long vowel. This lesson builds on the routines started in the Short Vowels lesson (pages 139–143).

Materials

- *Long Vowel Rime Charts* (pages 172–174); copy on cardstock and add one of each vowel to students' Short Vowel Rime Charts rings

Procedure

1. Say, "We have been learning about long vowels and different patterns for long vowels. Today, we are going to continue the chanting routine we use with short vowels and add long vowels to it."

2. Have students take out their Rime Charts rings with the newly added long vowels. Have students turn to the long *a* chart. Practice reading the patterns on the chart. For example, *ae, cake; ai, train; ay, play;* and OMG *eigh, weigh*.

3. Practice reading the long *a* chart each day until students are proficient. Then, move on to another vowel as it is introduced or as students are ready for it. Remember to go back and practice reading previously mastered charts as you proceed through the ring.

Cathy's Connections

Make sure students say, "The *e* makes the *a* say *a*," or "The *e* makes the *i* say *i*." Steer clear of the nonspecific rule, "The *e* makes the *o* say it's name." If you use the latter saying, you are creating a two-step rule. First, they have to know the *e* makes the *o* say "its name," then they have to know what that means. Many times when they are confused about this they'll say, "The *e* makes the *o* say its name," and then they'll make the short *o* sound. When we teach them to say, "The *e* makes the *o* say *o*," they are saying the sound they need to make.

Long Vowel Rime Charts

ā	ē
a__e – cake	ea – peach
ai – train	ee – tree
ay – play	ey – key
eigh – weigh	y – penny 2 syllables

Long Vowel Rime Charts *(cont.)*

ī	ō
 i__e – bike	 o__e – hose
ie – fries	 oa – boat
 igh – light	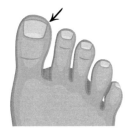 oe – toe
 y – sky 1 syllable/only vowel	 ow – row

124548—The Road to Independent Reading and Writing

Long Vowel Rime Charts *(cont.)*

ū

u__e – mule

ue – glue

ui – fruit

ew – blew

Long Vowel Rimes

Overview

Students practice various patterns for long vowels by matching pictures and writing words.

Materials

- *Long Vowel Rime Chart* for long *a* (page 172)
- student copies of *Long Vowel a Patterns* (page 176); enlarge to 200% for modeling
- student copies of *Long Vowel Patterns Pictures* (page 181); enlarge to 200% for modeling

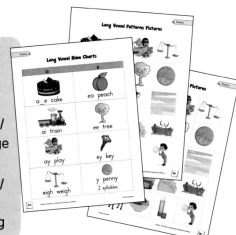

Procedure

1. Gather students on the carpet. Have students chant read the rimes and corresponding words on *Long Vowel Rime Chart* for long *a*.

2. Display the enlarged *Long Vowel a Patterns*. Guide students to recognize that the patterns on this chart are the same as on the chart they practice reading each day.

3. Say, "Today, we are going to create our own charts by looking at long *a* pictures and spelling the words using the patterns."

4. Display the *cake* picture card. Say the word *cake*, emphasizing the long *a* sound. Model how to glue the picture of the *cake* next to the *ae* pattern.

5. Tell students, "I can use the spelling pattern to help me spell the word. I hear /c/, I remember seeing the word *cake*, and I remember it starts with the letter *c*, so I will write *c*. Next, I hear /a/, so I will write *a*. I know it has to have a magic *e* for it to make the long vowel sound. I must remember to write that at the end. Next, I hear /k/, so I will write *k*. Finally, I will remember to write the silent *e*."

6. Repeat the process with the remaining pictures and patterns.

7. Provide students with their own copies of *Long Vowel a Patterns* and strips of *Long Vowel Patterns Pictures* for long *a*. Have them complete the activity by matching the pictures to their correct patterns and spelling the words.

Have students complete each *Long Vowel Pattern* sheet as you introduce each long vowel or as students are ready for it. Consider stapling all the pages together into a little book, so students have a personal resource to reference as they write. You can include the *Short Vowel Rimes* in the book, too! *Long Vowel Patterns Reference* (page 182) explains when each pattern is generally used.

Name _____

Long Vowel *a* Patterns

Directions: Glue each long vowel picture next to the correct spelling pattern. Write the words.

a_e		_____
ai		_____
ay		_____
eigh		_____

Long Vowel e Patterns

Directions: Glue each long vowel picture next to the correct spelling pattern. Write the words.

ea		
ee		
ey		
y 2 syllable word		

Long Vowel *i* Patterns

Directions: Glue each long vowel picture next to the correct spelling pattern. Write the words.

i_e		
ie		
igh		
y 1 syllable/only vowel		

Long Vowel o Patterns

Directions: Glue each long vowel picture next to the correct spelling pattern. Write the words.

o_e		
oa		
oe		
ow		

Long Vowel *u* Patterns

Directions: Glue each long vowel picture next to the correct spelling pattern. Write the words.

u_e		_____
ue		_____
ui		_____
ew		_____

Long Vowel Patterns Pictures

124548—The Road to Independent Reading and Writing

Long Vowel Patterns Reference

Long a	*a_e* (most of the time)	*ai* (in the middle of the word)	*ay* (usually at the end)	The OMG Pattern *eigh* (sounds like long *a*)
Long e	*ea* (usually in the middle of a word, but not always—*pea* or *sea*)	*ee* (can be at the end or in the middle)	*ey* (usually at the end of the word)	The OMG Pattern *y* (usually at the end of a two-syllable word)
Long i	*i_e* (most of the time)	*ie* (usually at the end)	*igh* (when *igh* are together the *gh* is always silent)	The OMG Pattern *y* (usually at the end of a one-syllable word when the *y* is the only vowel)
Long o	*o_e* (most of the time)	*oa* (usually when it's a long vowel sound in the middle of the word)	*oe* (usually at the end of the word)	The OMG Pattern *ow* (also at the end of the word, but *ow* can also sound like "OW, that hurts," so that's the OMG factor)
Long u	*u_e* (most of the time)	*ue* (usually at the end of the word, but can be in the middle)	*ui* (usually in the middle of the word)	The OMG Pattern *ew* (this combination can sound like a long *u* at the end of the word)

Every Q Needs a U—Day 1

Overview

This lesson takes place over four days. Students are introduced to the absolute of *q* and *u* as a spelling pattern, and then practice using it in a variety of activities.

Materials

- *Q Word Cards* (pages 184–185); cut apart
- *Q Absolutes Chart* (page 186)

Procedure

1. Gather students on the carpet. Say, "Today, I will show you some words that begin with the /kw/ sound." Show students two of the *Q Word Cards*.

2. Ask students to notice the beginning of each word and the letters they have in common. After they identify the *q* and *u* in both words, say, "Every *q* needs a *u*." It is fun to say this little rhyme with a British accent to make it fun. You can emphasize the letters as you say them, too. Have students repeat the rhyme as you point to the letters in the words.

3. Continue to show students the rest of the *Q Word Cards*, and have them identify the letters at the beginning of the words. For each card, ask students, "Why does this word start with *qu*?" Wait for their responses, and say, "Every *q* needs a *u*."

4. After working through all of the picture cards, ask students what they learned about words that begin with *q*. Make sure they respond with "Every *q* needs a *u*."

5. Display the *Q Absolutes Chart*. Read the chart together with students. Tell them this chart will be displayed in the room to help them remember that every *q* needs a *u*.

6. Conclude the lesson by saying, "We had so much fun today talking silly in order to remember that every *q* needs a *u*. We'll keep practicing tomorrow!"

Cathy's Connections

Admittedly, teaching phonics isn't the easiest thing to do. Unfortunately, many outdated practices are still in use today. Many teachers use the term *rule*, which can be confusing to students because they do not work 100% of the time. For example, many teachers will say, "when two vowels go walking, the first one does the talking"; however, that is not the case all the time. I believe we need to add words such as *most of the time* or *usually* when the rules we teach do not apply 100% of the time. Every *Q* needs a *U* is an absolute in English, and I teach it as such.

Q Word Cards

124548—The Road to Independent Reading and Writing

Q Word Cards (cont.)

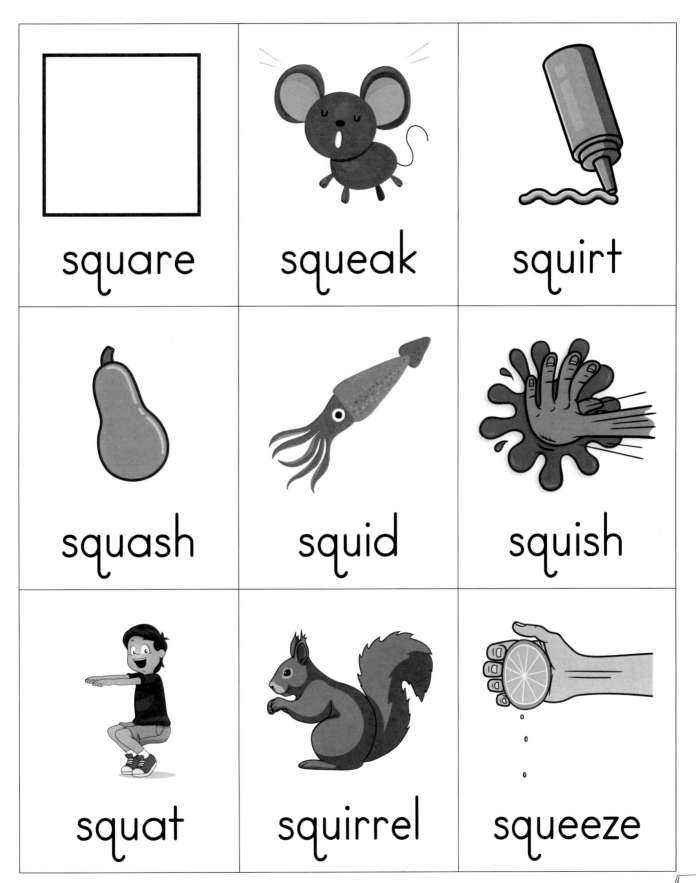

square	squeak	squirt
squash	squid	squish
squat	squirrel	squeeze

Q Absolutes Chart

Every q needs a u

quilt

quarter

queen

quiz

Every *Q* Needs a *U*—Day 2

Materials

- chart paper
- *Q Absolutes Chart* (page 186)
- *Q Picture Cards* (page 190)

Procedure

1. Seat students in view of the chart paper and the *Q Absolutes Chart*. Say, "Yesterday, we learned something very important about the letter *q*. What did we learn?" Wait for students to respond with "Every *q* needs a *u*."

2. Read the words on the *Q Word Cards*. Say, "Today, we are going to make sure we really understand what 'Every *q* needs a *u*' means. I'm going to ask for some volunteers to help me find *qu* on these picture cards."

3. Display the picture cards, one at a time. Have student volunteers circle the *qu* in each word on each chart. Every time the letters are circled, prompt students to say the rhyme, *Every q needs a u*. Be sure to point out that *qu* does not always have to be at the beginning of the word. Tape each picture card on the sheet of chart paper.

4. Say, "What a great day learning that every *q* needs a *u*. Now, I'm going to make some words, and you tell me if they follow our rule." Write some real and/or nonsense words on the board that contain *q* and *qu*. Ask students to give you a thumbs-up if a word follows the rule and a thumbs-down if it doesn't. Continue to prompt students to repeat the rhyme when a word follows the rule.

5. Tell students, "I'm so proud of you for remembering that 'Every *q* needs a *u*.' I can't wait for tomorrow when we keep practicing this rule."

Every Q Needs a U—Day 3

Materials

- chart paper
- *Q Absolutes Chart* (page 186)
- *Q Picture Cards* (page 190); cut apart
- student copies of *Spell Qu Words* (page 191)
- *student copies of Spell Qu Words Letter Cards* (page 192)

Procedure

1. Seat students in view of the chart paper and the *Q Absolutes Chart*. Ask, "What have we learned about the letter *q* in words?" Wait for students to respond with "Every *q* needs a *u*."

2. Say, "Today, we are going to write some words with the letter *q* in them." Show students the picture representing the word *quack* from *Q Picture Cards*. Ask them to tell you what the picture is. Ask them to say the word slowly and find the three word parts. Count with your fingers to illustrate stretching a word and finding the three word parts (/qu/ /a/ /k/).

3. Ask for a volunteer to identify the beginning sound /qu/ and spell how to make the sound. Have the student write the letters *q* and *u* on the chart paper.

4. Stretch the word again, and have another student identify the middle sound /ă/. Say, "I hear a short *a* sound, so it is probably an *a* all by itself. Who can write *a* on the chart?" Have a student volunteer write the letter *a* on the chart.

5. Finally, stretch the word again to hear the /k/ sound at the end of the word. Say, "The ending /k/ sound is beside the short *a*, so it is probably the letters *ck* together. If it was a /k/ sound beside a long *a*, then it would just be an ending *c* or an ending *k*." Ask a student volunteer to finish writing the word with the *c* and *k*.

6. Continue segmenting the word representing each picture card and having students record the spelling on the chart paper. Use the following prompts:

- **queen**—*qu*—Every *q* needs a *u*; *e*—the long *e* sound should mean two vowels together. It could be *ea* or *ee*. This time, the vowel pair is just like the word wall word see; *n*—the ending sound.

- **quick**—*qu*—Every *q* needs a *u*; *i*—It's a short vowel, so it's probably one letter; *ck*—Don't forget what we learned with quack. The short vowel sound is usually followed by the *ck*.

- **quiz**—*qu*—Every *q* needs a *u*; *i*—It's a short vowel, so it's probably one letter; *z*—I know that sound. It reminds me of *zipper*.

- **squid**—*s*—I hear a beginning sound /s/; *qu*—Every *q* needs a *u*; *i*—It's a short vowel, so it's probably one letter; *d*—I know that sound. It reminds me of *dog*.

- **squeak**—*s*—I hear a beginning sound /s/ like the beginning of *squid*; *qu*—Every *q* needs a *u*; I hear a long vowel *e*—this time, it's *ea*; finally, I hear a *k* like the beginning of *kite*.

Every *Q* Needs a *U*—Day 3 *(cont.)*

Procedure *(cont.)*

7. Distribute one copy of *Spell Qu Words* and a set of *Spell Qu Words Letter Cards* to each student. Tell students they get a chance to spell *qu* words by cutting apart the letter cards and gluing them in the correct order to spell the word the picture shows. Rotate around the room to monitor and assist students as they work.

8. Complete the lesson by saying, "What a fun day spelling *qu* words! Let's read all the words we built today."

This lesson also works well using magnetic letters on a board. Students can manipulate the letters to spell the words.

Q Picture Cards

Name _____

Spell Qu Words

Directions: Use the letter cards to spell each word.

Spell *Qu* Words Letter Cards

qu	qu	qu	qu	qu
qu	a	ea	ee	i
i	i	ck	ck	d
k	n	s	s	z

Every *Q* Needs a *U*—Day 4

Materials

- chart paper
- student copies of *The Quilt* (page 194); write the short story on chart paper for modeling

Procedure

1. Gather students on the carpet seated around the chart paper on which you have written the short story *The Quilt*.

2. Say, "We have been learning and playing with words with a *q*. What have we learned this week?" (Wait for the response: *Every q needs a u.*) Say, "Today, we are going to read a story and be detectives. As I read this story, listen and look for words that have *qu*." Read aloud the story to students.

3. Ask, "Who can be a detective and find a word with *qu* and circle it?" Ask for volunteers to circle *qu* in the words on the story chart. As students find each word, have them read the word aloud and write it at the bottom of the chart.

4. When all the words have been found, read the list at the bottom of the chart. Say, "You are great detectives! Now we know more *qu* words to read and write."

5. Model drawing a quick picture that illustrates the story.

6. Distribute copies of *The Quilt* to students. Tell them they get to circle all the *qu* words in the story in the first section. In the second section, they should write each *qu* word. Finally, in the third section, students can illustrate the story.

The Quilt

Directions: Circle the *qu* words in the story. Write the words. Draw a picture.

The Quilt

The queen saw a quilt at the market. The quilt cost her a quarter. She loved the quilt. She squeezed it, and it felt soft. It had squares with ducks quacking, squirrels eating nuts, and squids swimming. She was quick to put it on her bed. She slept all night and did not squirm.

Qu Words

Picture

Dr, Tr, Never, Ever Jr—Day 1

Overview

This lesson takes place over five days. Students often hear and spell *jr* for words with *dr* and *tr*. This lesson introduces students to a rhyme to help them remember the actual spelling and work on some follow-up activities to reinforce their learning.

Materials

- *Tr Chart* (page 196)
- *Dr Chart* (page 197)
- *Dr and Tr Word Cards* (page 198)

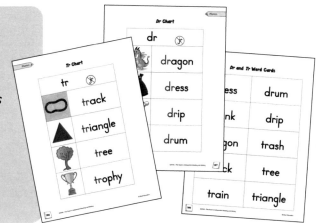

Procedure

1. Seat students in view of the *Dr Chart* and *Tr Chart*. Say, "We have been talking about rules that are rules and never change. We call these rules *absolutes*. This week, we will learn more absolutes. The rhyme to remind us is: *Dr, tr, never, ever jr.*" Have students repeat the rhyme.

2. Continue by saying, "When we are spelling words, we stretch them and write what we hear, but sometimes our ears trick us. If we remember *Dr, tr, never, ever jr*, it can help us listen more carefully and write the words correctly."

3. Point to the *Dr Chart and Tr Chart*, and say, "Look at the chart for these absolute spelling rules." Read the charts, and have students carefully listen and repeat the rhyme and the sounds.

4. Say, "Let's look at some word cards. Pay attention to the letters at the beginning of the words." Show students the word cards. Remind them of the absolute rule each time by saying, "*Dr, tr, never, ever jr.*"

5. Allow volunteers to circle the *dr* or *tr* at the beginning of each word on the word card, or write the words on a sheet of chart paper, and have volunteers circle the letters.

6. To complete the lesson, say, "Let's look at the absolutes chart once more today. When we want to write *jr*, we need to listen very carefully because now we know: *Dr, tr, never, ever jr.*"

Tr Chart

tr	(j̶r̶)
	track
	triangle
	tree
	trophy

Dr Chart

dr	(jr)
	dragon
	dress
	drip
	drum

Dr and *Tr* **Word Cards**

dress	drum
drink	drip
dragon	trash
track	tree
train	triangle

Dr, Tr, Never, Ever Jr—Day 2

Materials

- *Tr Chart* (page 196)
- *Dr Chart* (page 197)
- chart paper; draw a two-column chart and label one side *dr* and the other side *tr*
- *Dr and Tr Picture Cards* (page 200)

Procedure

1. Seat students in view of the *Dr* and *Tr Charts* and prepared chart paper. Review the chart, and ask students to tell you the absolute that they learned yesterday: *Dr, tr, never, ever jr.*

2. Say, "Today, we are going to sort some words by their beginning sounds. I'll leave our chart up, so we can make sure we hear those beginning sounds." Point out the two-column chart, and read the headers of each column.

3. Display a picture card on *Dr and Tr Picture Cards*, and have students name the picture card. Provide a definition if they don't know what the picture is. Ask students to listen to the beginning sound on the card. Work together to place the picture card in the correct column on the chart paper. As you do, have students chant, "*Dr, tr, never, ever jr.*"

4. Repeat the sorting routine with the other picture cards.

5. Say, "Look at our sort. Nice job listening to the beginning sounds. Now we know: *Dr, tr, never, ever jr.*"

Dr and Tr Picture Cards

Dr, Tr, Never, Ever Jr—Day 3

Materials

- *Tr Chart* (page 196)
- *Dr Chart* (page 197)
- chart paper
- *Dr and Tr Picture Cards* (page 200)
- student copies of *Spell Dr and Tr Words* (page 202)
- student copies of *Spell Dr and Tr Words Letter Cards* (page 203)

Procedure

1. Seat students around the chart paper. Ask, "What absolutes have we been working on?" (*Dr, tr, never, ever jr.*) Refer to the *Dr Chart* and *Tr Chart* as needed.

2. Say, "Today, we are going to write some words. Let's use what we know about words and sounds to write the words. Do you think you will hear a *dr, tr,* or a *jr*?" You want your students to react negatively to your suggestion of *jr*. They should know by now that it's *never, ever jr*.

3. Show students the picture representing the word *drag* on *Dr and Tr Picture Cards*. Ask them to tell you what the picture is. Have them say the word slowly. Count with your fingers to illustrate stretching a word (/dr/ /a/ /g/).

4. Ask for volunteers to write the beginning letters on the chart paper (*dr*). Stretch the word again, and have the next student add the *a*. Say, "I hear a short *a* sound, so it is probably an *a* all by itself." Finally, stretch the word again to hear the /g/ sound at the end of the word.

5. Continue segmenting the word representing each picture card and having volunteers record the spelling on the chart paper. Use the following prompts:

   - **trash**—*Dr, tr, never, ever jr; a* —It's a short vowel, so it's probably one letter; *sh* —the ending sound.
   - **trot**—*Dr, tr, never, ever jr; o* — It's a short vowel, so it's probably one letter; *t* —the ending sound.

   - **drill**—*Dr, tr, never, ever jr; i* —It's a short vowel, so it's probably one letter; *ll* —I remember to double the *l* at the end.
   - **truck**—*Dr, tr, never, ever jr; u* —It's a short vowel, so it's probably one letter; *ck* — Remember that sometimes the ending /k/ sound has two letters.
   - **dress**—*Dr, tr, never, ever jr; a* —It's a short vowel, so it's probably one letter; *ss* —I'll remember to double the *s* at the end.

6. Distribute one copy of *Spell Dr and Tr Words* and one copy of *Spell Dr and Tr Words Letter Cards* to each student. Tell students they get a chance to spell *dr* and *tr* words by cutting apart the letter cards and gluing them in the correct order to spell the word the picture shows. Rotate around the room to monitor and assist students as they work.

7. Complete the lesson by saying, "What a fun day spelling *dr* and *tr* words! Let's read all the words we built today."

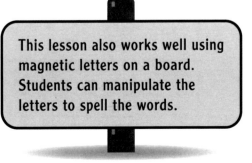

This lesson also works well using magnetic letters on a board. Students can manipulate the letters to spell the words.

Spell *Dr* and *Tr* Words

Directions: Use the letter cards to spell each word.

124548—The Road to Independent Reading and Writing

Spell *Dr* and *Tr* Words Letter Cards

dr	dr	dr	tr	tr
tr	a	a	o	i
u	e	ck	g	ll
sh	ss	t		

Dr, Tr, Never, Ever *Jr*—Day 4

Materials

- *Find the Treasure* (page 205); one copy per two students and one copy for modeling

Procedure

1. Say, "Who can remember what this week's absolute lesson has been about?" Wait for students to say: *Dr, tr, never, ever jr.*

2. Explain, "We have looked at words, sorted sounds, and even done some word building. Today, we are going to be detectives and find *dr* and *tr* in a story. I'm going to divide the class into teams of two to find the words in the story. BUT, there are rules. You will only have one marker for your team. Each person will take turns finding and circling the words in the story. I'll hand the marker to one partner, and they will go first. They will find a word, circle it, and hand the marker to their partner. You will take turns finding the words."

3. Place students into pairs, and distribute one copy of *Find the Treasure* and a marker to each pair. Allow time for students to work.

4. When students have finished, gather them back together. Have them sit with their partners and keep their papers. Say, "What a great job working with partners. I'm going to read this story to you. The first time you listen,

I want you to close your eyes and visualize what is happening. You can see it in your head while I read it. The story is called *Find the Treasure*, and it takes place on a beach. Do you have the setting in your head?" Read the story while students are listening with their eyes closed.

5. Display *Find the Treasure*. Then say, "Nice job listening to the story. Now, I want you to find the words on your papers as I read the story. When I get to a word you and your partner have circled, raise your hand, and I'll circle it on my paper." Read the story aloud, and circle the words on your paper as students raise their hands to tell you the words they circled.

6. Say, "Good work listening to the story today. Why do you think I wanted you to listen to it first with your eyes closed?" Accept several responses, and repeat any that focus on visualizing for understanding. Say, "You did a great job being word detectives. Tomorrow, we are going to write our own sentences using these words."

Cathy's Connections

When I have not previously had students do an activity such as circling words, I always like to model for students. In this lesson, before I sent students off to circle the words, I wrote a sentence or two on the board. I named two words in the sentences to circle. Next, I demonstrated how to draw a circle around each word. When drawing the circle, I described what I was doing and the size of circle I was making. Modeling like this before sending students to do the work independently will help to curtail any misunderstandings of what you want them to do, and in this case, will prevent unusually large or small circles!

Name _____

Find the Treasure

The pirate will draw a map for us to find treasure. We drive to the beach and follow the map past the triangle rock and the big tree. We have to stop for a drink and a dragonfly is flying around us. We find an X but a troll is there. We play a drum and a trumpet to scare him off. We dig and drag the treasure to our truck. What a dream.

Dr, Tr, Never, Ever Jr—Day 5

Materials

- *Missing Letter Word Cards* (page 207); cut apart
- writing paper

Procedure

1. Say, "Today, we are going to make words and write a sentence using the words. I am going to give each of you a word card with the beginning missing. You will decide on the beginning of the word, but I know you will choose *dr, tr*, never, ever *jr*."

2. Distribute a *Missing Letter Word Card* to each student. Be aware that some of the words have long vowels or ending blends. Differentiate which students you provide those cards to as needed. Ensure students make the words on their cards by adding the first two letters correctly.

3. Ask students to think of a sentence using their words. If students cannot think of a sentence, encourage them to use the sentence starters on the word wall. Have students orally practice their sentences with partners.

4. Distribute writing paper to students, and have them write the sentences they orally rehearsed. If time allows, have students illustrate their sentences. Say, "I'm loving the way everyone is making words and writing sentences. I can't wait for you to share these sentences."

5. Tell students, "I would like you to walk around the room and share your sentences with two different friends. You can read your sentences to each other. Make sure you tell your friends what a great job they did."

6. After students have shared with their friends, gather them back on the carpet. Have volunteers share a few sentences with the class, and congratulate them all on making good beginning sound choices. Say, "You wrote great sentences, and I loved your use of *dr* and *tr*. What did we learn?" Wait for them to say, "*Dr, tr*, never, ever *jr*."

Other absolutes are:

- when writing *–igh*, the *gh* is always silent
- *w* is always silent in *wr*
- *k* is always silent in *kn*

Missing Letter Word Cards

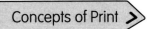
Concepts of Print

Concepts of print are students' understandings of how print is organized and read. Students with print awareness understand *how* to read a book before they can *actually* read the book. Print awareness ensures students know how to hold the book, where to move with words, and the difference between a letter and a word; therefore, the focus can be clearly on learning to read. To be successful readers, students need to understand the following concepts:

- Print has meaning.
- Print is read from left-to-right, top-to-bottom, and front-to-back.
- Print contains letters, words, and sentences.
- Print has conventions that involve capitals, spaces, and end marks.

Explicitly teaching and then reinforcing concepts of print can be easily incorporated during read-alouds, with the teacher asking simple questions, such as "Where is the front cover of the book?" or "Where do I start to read?" More specific lessons can be targeted in small groups as needed. Concepts of print are more easily practiced with simple exposure to texts.

Print Concepts	Examples
Overall Text Concepts	Understanding of the concept of a book, which way to hold it, that books contain words and pictures that communicate meaning, and that the content of the book remains constant
Text Directionality	Text is read from left-to-right, top-to-bottom, and each word is read
Text Understandings	Written words represent spoken words, words are made of letters that represent sounds, spaces separate words
Text Orientation	Books need to be held upright, letters have directionality, pages are sequenced and turned from left-to-right
Parts of a Book	Books contain a front cover, back cover, spine, author's name, illustrator's name, and other components, such as tables of contents or indexes

Print Awareness—Day 1

Overview

This lesson takes place over five days. Students explore print concepts through the use of the words to the familiar and beloved tune, "Twinkle, Twinkle."

Materials

• *Twinkle, Twinkle* chart (page 210); enlarge to 200%

Procedure

1. Gather students together on the carpet. Sing the song "Twinkle, Twinkle." After singing, display the *Twinkle, Twinkle* chart. Tell students the chart has the words to the song they just sang. Tell them they will sing the song again. Say, "This time, I will point to the words on the chart as we sing the song."

2. Point to the title of the poem, and say, "This is the title or name of the poem." Then, point to the first line of the poem, and say, "Here is where we will start singing." Have students say, "Always start at the top." Point to the words as students sing the song again.

3. Choose a student volunteer to come help you point to the words as the group sings the song once again. Using a special pointer with a star can be an exciting connection for students.

4. After singing, say, "Today, we sang a song we already knew, but we also pointed to words as we sang it. We made sure to start at the top of the paper, and we followed the words down the paper as we went."

Twinkle, Twinkle

Twinkle, twinkle, little star.

How I wonder what you are.

Up above the world so high,

Like a diamond in the sky.

Twinkle, twinkle, little star.

How I wonder what you are.

Print Awareness—Day 2

Materials

- *Twinkle, Twinkle* chart (page 210)

Procedure

1. Gather students on the carpet. Display the *Twinkle, Twinkle* chart, and say, "Yesterday, we sang the song and read the song. Where did we start when we were reading?" (*top*) Say, "Today, we are going to talk about moving from left-to-right and from top-to-bottom. Let's read the poem together, starting at the top.

2. After you begin, stop after reading the word *star* on the first line. Say, "I think I forget what to do when I get to the end of a line. Should I go down one line and read it back to the front (reading right-to-left), or should I jump back to the left and read it from there (reading left-to-right). I'm just not sure. Can anyone help me?"

3. After students respond with the correct answer, say, "I have an idea. Let's try it both ways to see if we are correct. First, I'll get to the end and just go to the line under and move back. Here goes. Twinkle, twinkle, little star. are you what wonder I How. Hmmm, that does not sound right. Let me try it the other way." Jump back to the beginning of the line. Say, "Twinkle, twinkle, little star. How I wonder what you are. Does that sound right to you?" Allow students to respond. "Yay! I think we figured it out."

4. Say, "Let's go back and read the poem now that we all know to jump back to the beginning at the end of each line." Reread the poem several times, asking for student volunteers to point to the words as the group reads it.

5. Say, "Today, we read the poem and practiced jumping from the end of each line back to the beginning of the next line to keep reading."

Print Awareness—Day 3

Materials

- *"Twinkle, Twinkle"* chart (page 210)
- tongue depressors or slips of paper; write each of the Print Awareness Questions on one and place in a jar or other holder
- *Print Awareness Questions* (page 213)
- crayons

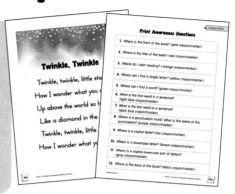

Procedure

1. Seat students in full view of the *"Twinkle, Twinkle"* chart. Guide them to review what they practiced with the poem in the previous lessons (read top-to-bottom, left-to-right, and a return sweep). Say, "Today, we are going to be print detectives. What do you think that means?" Listen to student responses, then ask students to tell you what a detective does (looks for clues and solves problems). Ask students what they think a print detective will do. (Look for clues and solve problems with print.)

2. Say, "I have questions written in my jar. These questions are about print features we can find in the print of our "Twinkle, Twinkle" poem. I will pull a question and choose one of you to be my print detective. You can use my magnifying glass and look for clues in the poem to solve the problem."
   Note: Two of the questions (*Where is the front of the book?* and *Where is the back of the book?*) cannot be used with a chart and should only be used with a book.

3. Choose a question, read it, and ask a student volunteer to find the answer in the poem. Questions can be color-coded, and students can use the colors to "solve the mystery" by marking the text. For example, when asking a print detective to find a specific letter, the print detective can circle the letter with a yellow crayon.
   Note: If you would like students to circle their answers with their fingers first and then use the marker, errors on the chart will be limited.

4. Continue choosing questions and students to respond. End the lesson by saying, "You are definitely print detectives! What are some of the print features we found today in the poem?"

Print Awareness Questions

1. Where is the front of the book? (pink crayon/marker)

2. Where is the title? (red crayon/marker)

3. Where do I start reading? (orange crayon/marker)

4. Where can I find a single letter? (yellow crayon/marker)

5. Where can I find a word? (green crayon/marker)

6. What is the first word in a sentence?
   (light blue crayon/marker)

7. What is the last word in a sentence?
   (dark blue crayon/marker)

8. Where is a punctuation mark? What is the name of the punctuation mark? (purple crayon/marker)

9. Where is a capital letter? (tan crayon/marker)

10. Where is a lowercase letter? (brown crayon/marker)

11. Where is a capital-lowercase pair of letters?
    (gray crayon/marker)

12. Where is the back of the book? (black crayon/marker)

Print Awareness—Days 4 and 5

Materials

- *Twinkle, Twinkle* chart (page 210)
- "*Twinkle, Twinkle, Little Star*" Book (pages 216–219); copy and assemble one per student
- *Print Detective Badges* (page 219); one per student
- crayons

Procedure

1. Begin the lesson by reviewing the *Twinkle, Twinkle* chart. Ask students to review some of the print features they discovered when they were print detectives. Say, "If we look at all the colors on our chart, we can see all the print features we found in our poem! Knowing all these print features helps us focus on learning the words and understanding what is written."

2. Say, "Today, we are going to be print detectives again, but this time, we will be using a book. I have made a "Twinkle, Twinkle, Little Star" book for you! Let's use our crayons to find print features in this book." With students at their desks, pass out the books, making sure to put them randomly upside down and backward in front of students.

3. Once students have their books, ask them to orient them correctly, so they are ready to read. Turn the print awareness questions into commands. For example, say, "Take out your pink crayon, and find the front of your book. Once you have the front of your book, make a large rectangle around the outside edge of the cover." Walk around the room and monitor students. Say, "Now, find the back of the book. Write your name with black crayon on the back."

4. Continue with directions for students to find print features and use crayons to mark specific features. Guide students to mark and find six of the print features, directing them to circle, underline, or put an asterisk by them.

Note: Some pages lend themselves to specific print features. For example, using pages 1, 2, 5, or 6 for the capital-lowercase match can help students circle a capital *T* and lowercase *t*, or a capital *H* and lowercase *h* on the same page.

5. Complete the lesson by saying, "Today, we started being print detectives in our book. I can't wait to finish this tomorrow."

6. On Day 5, complete the final six print feature questions (changed to commands) using the same procedure.

7. Once the book is complete, have student pairs read their books with one another.

8. Distribute *Print Detective Badges* to students. Have them color and cut out the badges to wear. Say, "This has been a fun week. Being a print detective is a fun and interesting way to learn about print features that will help you when you read. Great job!"

Print Awareness—Days 4 and 5 *(cont.)*

Cathy's Connections

I don't believe we should "dumb down" vocabulary with students. I don't believe in "boo-boo tape." Instead, we should call it "editing tape" because it's for editing, not for boo-boos. Boo-boos hurt. I don't think we should tell students made-up, "easy-to-understand" names when we can just tell them the real words and make them mean something valuable. Tell students they are going to learn about *print features* because that's what they are. Later, they will learn about *text features* and can make the connection to *print features*.

"Twinkle, Twinkle, Little Star" Book

Twinkle, Twinkle

Twinkle, twinkle, little star.

"Twinkle, Twinkle, Little Star" Book *(cont.)*

How I wonder what you are!

Up above the world so high,

"Twinkle, Twinkle, Little Star" Book *(cont.)*

Like a diamond in the sky.

Twinkle, twinkle, little star.

"Twinkle, Twinkle, Little Star" Book *(cont.)*

How I wonder what you are!

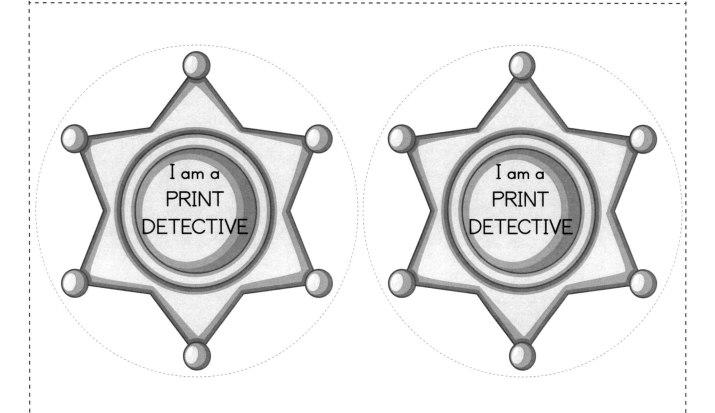

Concept of Word—Day 1

Overview

This three-day routine helps students develop the concept of a word. The routine can be moved into an intervention by using poems and nursery rhymes. Students should have a "working knowledge" of the poem.

Materials

- *"I Like Apples" Poem* (page 225; see sidebar as well)
- *I Like Apples Picture Cards* (page 221; see Digital Resources for a color version); cut apart

Procedure

1. Seat students on the carpet. Display the *I Like Apples Picture Cards* vertically, so each picture represents one line of the poem. Say, "Today, we are going to practice a poem." Read aloud the *I Like Apples* poem to students. Point to the corresponding picture card as you say each line of the poem.

2. Reread the poem having students echo each line after you read it, pointing to the picture cards as the lines are read.

3. Read aloud each line of the poem and work together to determine a hand motion to help them remember the poem.

4. Practice the poem with the hand motions several times. Allow student volunteers to point to the pictures as each line is recited.

5. End the lesson by saying, "Nice job today repeating the poem while we matched our words to the pictures."

I Like Apples

I like to pick some apples.

So wonderful to eat.

Apple pie and apple sauce

And a yummy treat.

I Like Apples Picture Cards

124548—The Road to Independent Reading and Writing **221**

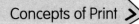

Concept of Word—Day 2

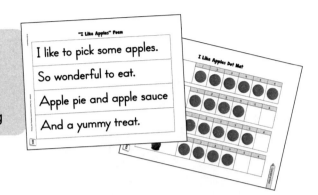

Materials

- *"I Like Apples" Poem* (page 225)
- student copies of *I Like Apples Dot Mat* (page 223); enlarge to 200% for modeling

Procedure

1. Gather students on the carpet, and display the enlarged *I Like Apples Dot Mat*. Say, "Yesterday, we said our poem just using pictures. Today, we're just going to point to a dot to represent each word we say. I have included the pictures at the beginning of the line to remind us. Let me show you how to point to the dots and say the words." Recite the *I Like Apples* poem aloud for students. As you do, point to one dot for each word you say.

2. Allow student volunteers to come point to the dots as the class recites the poem several more times.

3. Distribute copies of *I Like Apples Dot Mat* to students. Have them touch each dot as they practice reciting the poem. This can be done as a whole class or in pairs. Monitor students who may need additional practice with you in a small group.

4. Say, "I love the way we matched our dots with words when we were saying our poem. We had to be careful about words with two-parts or two-part syllables, such as *yummy* and *apples*, and our three-syllable word *wonderful*. How many dots do we touch when we say the word *pick*?" Wait for the response (*one*) "How many dots do we touch when we say the word *yummy*?" Wait for the response (*one*). "Correct. How many dots do we touch when we say the word *wonderful*?" Wait for the response (*one*).

5. End the lesson by saying, "Excellent job matching our dots with words today."

I Like Apples Dot Mat

	1	2	3	4	5	6
	●	●	●	●	●	●
	●	●	●	●		
	●	●	●	●	●	
	●	●	●	●		

Concept of Word—Day 3

Materials

- *I Like Apples Poem* (page 225); enlarged to 200% and cut into strips or written on sentence strips
- *I Like Apples Dot Mat* (page 223)
- scissors

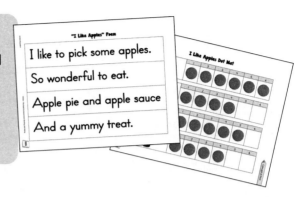

Procedure

1. Gather students on the carpet. Display the "I Like Apples" poem. Say, "We have been digging deep in our poem this week. We said the poem with only pictures, and we said the poem as we touched a dot for each word. Today, we are going to look at the words. We only have words, no pictures, no dots. We have to remember to touch one word at a time. Let's do it together."

2. Recite the poem with the class as you point to one word at a time. Repeat several times.

3. Next, cut the first sentence strip into individual word cards. There should be six word cards. Distribute the word cards to six volunteers. Refer back to the *I Like Apples Dot Mat* from yesterday's lesson. Say, "Now that we cut the sentence apart, let's put it back together. Let's point to the dots and say the sentence." Point to the dots as the class recites the first line of the poem.

4. Have students repeat the first line, and ask the volunteers to put the words in order. When the words are in order, ask students to find a word in the sentence. Say, "Now that the sentence is back together, can anyone find the word *like*?"

5. Repeat with each sentence of the poem, cutting, distributing the words, putting it back together, and asking students to find a word in each sentence.

6. Conclude the lesson by saying, "You did a great job today. It is always important to have the words put in order so it makes sense."

I like to pick some apples.

So wonderful to eat.

Apple pie and apple sauce

And a yummy treat.

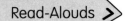

Read-Aloud Planning

Read-alouds are by definition books read aloud to your students, but it isn't just about reading the book. It's about showing students how they can be entertained by books and learn from books. Reading aloud can include lessons on story elements, story comprehension, author discussions, vocabulary, and everything else in reading. One of the most offensive things you can do to start a lesson is take a book off the shelf and hope it will make sense to your readers and for the lesson. Reading aloud can be the highlight of the day if you take a few minutes to plan and preread the book. Here are some considerations for planning.

1. Plan Think-Alouds

Books can be read for entertainment, but if you are reading for a purpose, make a plan. Using sticky notes is an easy way to leave notes for yourself. Jotting down key words on the sticky note or listing questions for your students at each place in the book can create an intentional read. Deciding where to pause for emphasis or understanding and where you need to paraphrase or add an explanation to ensure understanding can allow students to get the most from the story. For example, *Stellaluna* by Janell Cannon is a great way to teach compare and contrast. *Stellaluna* is different from her bird "brothers and sisters," but they had some things in common, as well. Knowing you are going to teach compare and contrast during the read-aloud helps you engage your students in the book and make connections.

2. Plan Vocabulary

So many teachers and students love the Magic Tree House books by Mary Pope Osborne. I could probably teach any skill using these books, and they are great for vocabulary, as well. We read a Magic Tree House book in 11 days. The first day is all about vocabulary, then it's a chapter a day with summaries, predictions, and fun. During the introduction day, we discuss any vocabulary students may need to fully understand the book. In the book, *The Knight at Dawn*, we discuss the difference between *night* and *knight*, the words relating to castles (i.e., *great hall*, *dungeon*, *armory*, and more), and the word *precipice*, which will become an integral part of the plot. We define it, model it, and own it before we read the book. Then, when we are reading, the vocabulary doesn't stop comprehension.

3. Practice Rhythm

Some books need practice. *The Three Ninja Pigs* by Corey Rosen Schwartz is a great retelling of *The Three Little Pigs*. It is fun, and students love the story. However, the entire book is written in limerick. You will need to practice the rhythm of the book ahead of time so students will be able to enjoy the rhythm and the story.

4. Practice Story Language

Flossie & the Fox by Patricia C. McKissack is one of my favorite books. It is a retelling of *Little Red Riding Hood*, but it is set in the South and is written using an old southern dialect. There are examples of nonstandard English, so students need to understand the story language so it doesn't affect comprehension or the entertainment value of the story.

> "All due respect, Miz Cat, but both y'all got sharp claws and yellow eyes. So... that don't prove nothing, cep'n both y'all be cats."
> —Patricia C. McKissack

Read-Aloud Planning *(cont.)*

5. Understand Emotions

This area of planning is special to me because I made the classic mistake of not prereading the book *Chicken Sunday* by Patricia Polacco before I read it to my students. I had ordered the book years ago and was so excited to read it when I got it, I didn't preread the book. This is truly one of my favorite books, but by the end of the story, I was crying. Yep. Crying. My emotions were slowly building with the friendship of the three main characters, the story of Mr. Kodinski's shop and his back story, the disappointment on Miss Eula's face, and how the children decide to help Mr. Kodinski when they didn't have to. But at the end, it says, "Winston, Stuart, and I are all grown up now. We lost Miss Eula some time back, but every year we take some chicken soup up to Mountain View Cemetery and do just what she asked."

Oh, goodness. I'm tearing up just writing this. So trust me, preread so you don't start the "snurping cry" in front of your students.

6. Anything Objectionable?

Finally, this is one of my favorite reasons to preread the book. A book was in our teacher resource library, but one day a frantic teacher came to me and asked me to have the book removed from the book room. She had not preread the book, and she had shared it with her second graders. The book was a standard retelling of *Little Red Riding Hood*, but it's a little "real." In it, the huntsman slices the belly of the wolf with his axe to help Grandma and Little Red out of his belly. Grandma is a little rattled by the close quarters of the wolf belly, so she has a glass of wine. (Yep, the wine and bottle are in the illustration!) The huntsman takes home the pelt of the wolf to hang on his wall. Needless to say, prereading is important!

Note: I didn't take it out of the resource library. Instead, I put a "warning" label on the cover.

I hope I have inspired you to preread the books you read aloud to your students. This will ensure you make the most of the story, showcase quality writing, and capitalize on your instruction.

Cathy's Connections

I believe in rereading books. A book shouldn't be put in the "cause-and-effect" section of the library and never used again. What if that book is great for drawing conclusions, too? What if there is a great example of an inference in chapter three of a book you have already read? Use it! Bring the book to the carpet, and say, "Boys and girls, I have something exciting today. Look at what book we are going to use today." Hold up the already-read book. "Yes, we have already read this book, but today, I'm only going to read a small part of the book because I think it contains something we are talking about." Remind students of the story and what was happening up to the highlighted passage. Reread the section of the book with the relevant example. Don't get stuck in the cycle of rereading the whole book.

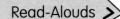

Read-Aloud Checklist

Read-alouds are an integral part of many lessons. Drawing connections between lessons, stories, characters, events, and students' lives can make all the difference in the world. Planning for experiences and lessons before, during, and after the book can solidify these connections.

Before Reading

1. Activate Prior Knowledge—Relate the story to known characters, series, or themes.

2. Set a Purpose—Make sure students know why they are listening to the story.

3. Introduce the Book—Give a short two or three sentence introduction to the text. Make sure to mention characters and settings, if they are necessary for understanding or predicting.

4. Define Vocabulary Words—Some words can be defined in the context of the story, but some must be explained before reading so as to not disrupt meaning in the story.

5. Make Predictions—Allow students to look at pictures to make predictions. Make sure they can justify their predictions.

During Reading

1. Read with expression and fluency.

2. Model thinking aloud.

3. Make connections throughout the story to allow students to relate the story to themselves, another text, the world, or media.

4. Make inferences about what the author is saying, or draw conclusions about what will happen next.

5. Highlight new vocabulary words as you read them.

6. Confirm and revise predictions with proof or evidence from the text.

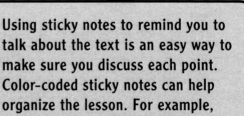

Using sticky notes to remind you to talk about the text is an easy way to make sure you discuss each point. Color-coded sticky notes can help organize the lesson. For example, yellow for vocabulary, blue for summary, and green for connections.

After Reading

1. Retell the story, making sure to include the characters, setting, and events. The "Somebody-Wanted-But-So-And-Then" model (see Summarizing, pages 270–274 can help students retell the whole story.

2. Identify the main idea (nonfiction) or theme (fiction) in the story.

3. Continue to make connections to the text.

4. Comprehension should be at many levels, from surface level to deeper comprehension. Students should be able to understand ideas about the text and beyond the text.

5. Review vocabulary words, and ask students to relate and recall the vocabulary from the text.

6. Allow students to confirm and revise predictions with proof.

Asking Questions—Day 1

Overview

This lesson is taught to students over two days. Students are asked to understand and use comprehension strategies. Students practice asking questions about what they are reading.

Materials

- *Asking Questions* chart (page 230; see Digital Resources for a color version)
- mentor text (*Stellaluna* by Janell Cannon is used in this lesson)

Procedure

1. Display the *Asking Questions* chart. Read the words to students, and model asking students a question for each word. For example, *"Who* is 5 years old in this class?" Students will certainly raise hands and have answers. Explain to students that questions have to be answered.

2. Look at the cover of a mentor text, for example, *Stellaluna*. Say, "Today, we are going to read a new book. Let's look at the cover and ask questions." Ask students questions about the cover. Samples of questions:

   - *Who* is Stellaluna?
   - *Where* does Stellaluna live?
   - *What* could be the problem in the story?
   - *What* do I know about bats?
   - *When* does the story take place?
   - *Why* is Stellaluna hanging on that branch as if she doesn't know how to fly?
   - *How* does the story end?

3. Tell students you will only read a few pages today to see if any of the questions posed are answered. Read the first three pages of the book. Then, stop to think about if any questions have been answered by the text. If a question is answered, model posing a new question based on the answered question. For example, say, "I see we have answered the question, *Who is Stellaluna?*. We now know that Stellaluna is the bat who is lost, but that makes me wonder how Stellaluna lives without her mother."

> A *mentor text* is any book or other type of text, such as a poem or song, used to study as students learn about reading and writing.

Cathy's Connections

Every teacher has had that moment when they ask, "Does anyone have a question?" and a student raises their hand to *tell* you something. This can be addressed in this lesson or in a game. With a washable marker, draw a question mark on each students' right hand and a period on their left hand. Tell students you want them to distinguish between questions and statements with their hands, not their mouths. Tell them when you make a statement, they should raise their left hand. When you ask a question, they should raise their right hand. This is a fun way for students to listen for target words and inflection.

Asking Questions

Readers
ask questions.

Who?   When?

What?   How?

Where?   Why?

Asking Questions—Day 2

Materials

- mentor text (*Stellaluna* by Janell Cannon is used in this lesson)
- *Asking Questions* chart (page 230)
- *Asking Questions Anchor Chart Pieces* (pages 233–234); cut pieces apart

Procedure

1. Show students the book, *Stellaluna*, and review the *Asking Questions* chart from yesterday. Say, "Yesterday, we asked questions about what might be in the book. Strong readers ask questions about what they are reading to understand a story. Today, we are going to make an anchor chart to help us remember to ask questions."

2. Distribute *Asking Questions Anchor Chart Pieces* to students. Work with students to assemble the pieces on a sheet of chart paper. Say, "Let's start with the title. If you have a piece of the title, come up, and let's put it on the top of the chart." Have the student with the title bring it up and glue it at the top of the chart.

3. Say, "Next, let's add the words telling us how to be readers." Have the student with the piece about what readers do glue it to the chart paper.

4. Then say, "Let's add the girl. She is asking a question. Above her head is a question mark, and we add that to our questions to show we are asking something. We will be adding those to our writing this year. We also know when we are reading questions because that symbol makes our voice go up and come down, just like the symbol."

5. Finally say, "Let's add the question words." Have students with the six question words glue them to the chart. Review the student-created anchor chart with students.

6. Finish reading the book *Stellaluna*. As you are reading, make sure to stop and ask and answer questions aloud. Reference the student-created anchor chart as you do. After the story, say, "You are very good at asking questions about stories because you are readers."

7. Continue to read other mentor texts and practice asking and answering questions.

Asking Questions—Day 2 *(cont.)*

Cathy's Connections

Creating anchor charts with students, such as the *Asking Questions* chart described in this lesson, helps them invest in the concept depicted on the chart. Participation in the process makes it likely that students will retain the information on the chart and reference it as it is displayed in the room. Each of the reading strategies provided in this section has a mini chart for teacher use. (A color version is provided in the Digital Resources.) Pieces for a larger anchor chart are also provided in the Digital Resources so you can work with your students to make a student-created anchor chart. Follow a procedure similar to the one described in this lesson to assemble the anchor charts with students. For additional tips about anchor charts, see pages 11–12.

Asking Questions Anchor Chart Pieces

Asking Questions

Readers ask questions about what they are reading.

Asking Questions Anchor Chart Pieces *(cont.)*

Where? | What?

Who? | When?

Why? | How?

Making Connections

Overview

Students practice making connections with text by making connections to themselves, to another text, to the world, or to media.

Materials

- mentor text (*I Went Walking* by Sue Williams is used in this lesson)
- *Making Connections* chart (page 237; see Digital Resources for a color version)

Procedure

1. Start the lesson with a mentor text that has been read to students before. Say, "Students, I remember this book. We read it last week. I enjoyed it, so I decided to read it again."

2. Continue by saying, "Readers reread texts all the time. We read it better the second time. We understand it better and can enjoy it because we already know about the book. We know the vocabulary, characters, and events. We can also make connections to the text. When we make connections, we decide how we can connect or put together something in the book with something we know."

3. Display the *Making Connections* chart. Say, "Today, as we enjoy this book, I am going to show you how I can make connections throughout the story. Briefly explain each of the types of connections that can be made when reading.

4. Start reading the book. Stop at a point where you can model one of the connections. For example, after reading a few pages of *I Went Walking*, you could stop and say, "If I look at my four connections pictures, I know I can make a text or book connection to this page because I have read other books with cats, such as *If You Give a Cat a Cupcake*."

5. Continue reading, stopping as you are able to make connections, such as "Here is a connection to myself that I can make. When I was on vacation last summer, we saw a lot of ducks in the pond where we were fishing."

6. Finish reading the story as you continue to make connections. Attempt to make all four connections the first time you model making connections.

7. Say, "This is certainly a new way to read a book. Honestly, it's hard to make all those connections in one book and still enjoy the book. Stopping so much can be tricky. Normally, I wouldn't make all the connections in one book, but I wanted you to see how to use this strategy."

8. Continue to read other mentor texts and practice making connections on subsequent days.

Making Connections *(cont.)*

Cathy's Connections

This is a seemingly easy skill, but we can't let this be the depth of our comprehension discussion. Too many teachers rely on "What connection can you make to this story?" during comprehension, and it just isn't digging deep enough. It is part of your comprehension arsenal, but it's not the only piece.

See the Digital Resources for pieces to make a student-created anchor chart for Making Connections. See pages 231–234 for a sample lesson on how to build an anchor chart with students.

Making Connections

Readers make connections to things they already know.

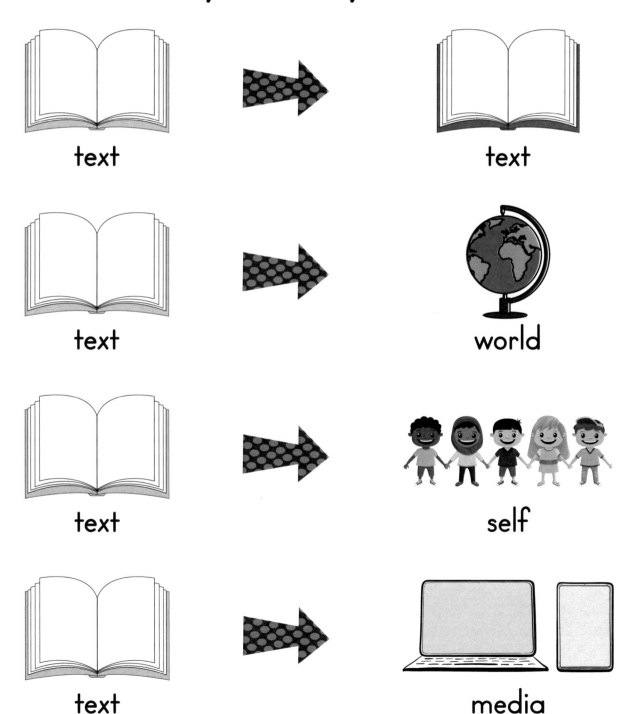

text   →   text

text   →   world

text   →   self

text   →   media

Visualizing—Day 1

Overview

This lesson is taught to students over four days. Students are asked to understand and use comprehension strategies. Students practice visualizing what is happening or being described in a text.

Materials

- student copies of *Visualize a Pool* (page 239; cut apart)
- *Visualize* chart (page 240; see Digital Resources for a color version)

Procedure

1. Explain to students what it means to visualize. Say, "Students, we are going to be talking about visualizing today. You have probably never heard that word, but I bet you have all been to the doctor and they have checked your eyes. They might have put a cover over one eye and asked you to tell them what you see on a chart. Then, they switched the cover to the other eye and asked you again. Right?" Wait for nods of agreement. Say, "That was a vision test. Every time you hear the word *vision* or *visual* or *visualizing*, it means you use your eyes."

2. Continue explaining by saying, "So, now let's talk about visualizing when we are reading. Visualizing isn't about seeing the words or the pictures, it's about seeing the story in your mind when you read."

3. Distribute copies of *Visualize a Pool* to students, and tell them, "Close your eyes, and think of a kiddie swimming pool. Think about what color the pool is. Keep your eyes closed. Now, let's say there is a float in the pool. I need you to think about what color that float is. When you open your eyes, I want you to color the pool and float pictures on your paper." Allow students time to color their pictures.

4. Call students to the carpet with their pictures. Say, "I want you to share with your carpet partner. What color was the pool in your mind? What color was the float?" Give students time to talk to their friends. When they are finished, ask a few student volunteers to share how they had visualized the pool and the float.

5. Say, "Can anyone tell me why the pictures on your paper might be on sunglasses?" Wait for student responses. Say, "We are using sunglasses because visualizing is all about what we *see* just like sunglasses."

6. Display and discuss the *Visualize* chart. Say, "When we visualize, we put a picture in our head about what is happening in the story. This chart can remind us to think about the story while we read by putting a picture in our mind. I didn't give you many details, so you had to make your own choices. You did a great job visualizing today."

> **See the Digital Resources for pieces to make a student-created anchor chart for Visualizing. See pages 231–234 for a sample lesson on how to build an anchor chart with students.**

Visualize a Pool

Directions: Color the pool and float the way you visualized it.

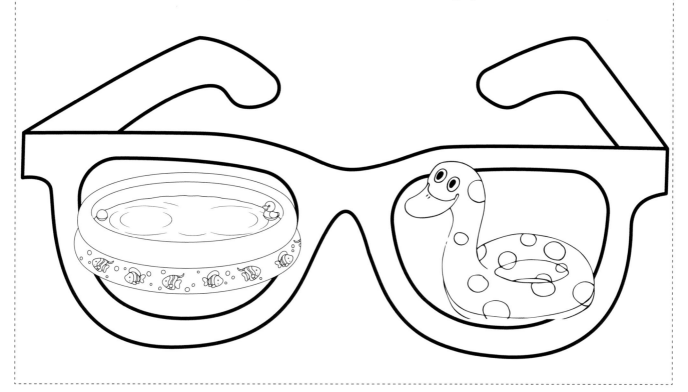

Directions: Color the pool and float the way you visualized it.

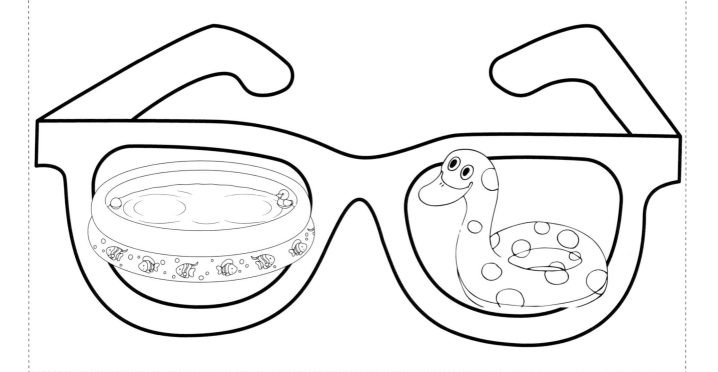

Visualize

Readers make pictures in their heads when they are reading.

124548—The Road to Independent Reading and Writing

Visualizing—Day 2

Materials

- *Visualize* chart (page 240)
- *Visualizing Pictures* (page 242; see Digital Resources for a color version)

Procedure

1. Remind students, "Strong readers visualize. They make a picture in their heads when they read." Review the *Visualize* chart and yesterday's lesson. If you would like to add a visualizing cue, use your index finger and point back and forth between your eyes and your brain.

2. Say, "Today, we are going to visualize some more. As I read a passage, you will close your eyes and visualize what I am reading. When I am finished reading, you will open your eyes and tell me which of the two pictures you had in your head. Let's try it." Have students close their eyes. As their eyes are closed, display the pictures for *Story 1* from *Visualizing Pictures*. Read *Story 1* from the box below.

3. When the story is finished, ask students to keep their eyes closed and spend a few more seconds to get a very clear picture in their heads. Say, "Before you open your eyes, let me think about the story one more time. I could see things that remind me of Thanksgiving, maybe a person. I also heard about a hat and a buckle, so I'm seeing that in my mind, too. But the thing that really makes me think is when I read about feathers. Hmmm? *Thanksgiving. Buckle. Hat. Feathers.* Open your eyes, and let's look at the pictures. Which picture was I talking about?"

4. Listen for student reactions. Ask students if the picture in their minds looked like the picture they see in front of them. Say, "When I was reading, I thought we were talking about a Pilgrim until I heard the part about the feathers. Who else had that happen to the picture in their mind? The great thing about reading and visualizing is that what we visualize will change as we read. It helps us better understand the story."

5. Tell students they will practice visualizing again. Ask students to close their eyes. Display the pictures for *Story 2* from *Visualizing Pictures*. Read *Story 2* from the box below. Follow the same procedure as before, and check their visualizations.

6. Say, "I am very impressed with your visualizing today. Closing our eyes really helps us focus on making a picture in our heads. Why is it important to visualize when we are reading?" Listen for answers, but make sure they know, "Strong readers make pictures in their heads when they read to help them understand the story."

Story 1	Story 2
You see me at Thanksgiving. I have on a tall, brown hat with a big buckle on the front. I also have feathers.	I found a treasure chest. It is marked with a pirate flag. I am standing on the chest.

Visualizing Pictures

Story 1

Story 2

Visualizing—Day 3

Materials

- *Visualize* chart (page 240)
- dry erase boards and markers; 1 per student

Procedure

1. Display the *Visualize* chart, and ask students what it tells us about being readers. Make sure they answer, "Readers make pictures in their heads when they read." Review the activity and stories from Day 2.

2. Distribute dry erase boards and markers to students. Say, "Today, we are going to play a new game with visualizing. I am going to give you the directions for writing a letter, but I'm not going to tell you what letter I'm making. I'm only going to give you the directions."

3. Have students close their eyes. Ask them to visualize a sheet of paper and a pencil. They are going to move the pencil on the paper as you read directions. Say, "Draw a straight line down, and then draw a straight line across the top." Repeat the directions several times, providing time for students to visualize what you are saying.

4. Have students open their eyes and follow the directions by drawing what they visualized on their dry erase boards. Repeat the directions again as students draw. Ask students, "What letter did we form?" Wait for responses.

5. Continue the procedure as you give directions for other letters.

6. Say, "Great job today using visualizing to help you write letters. We know visualizing helps us make a picture in our head while we are reading or listening. Visualizing helps us understand better."

Visualizing—Day 4

Materials
- *Visualize* chart (page 240)
- drawing paper
- mentor text

Procedure

1. Gather students on the carpet. Review the previous day's activities and the *Visualize* chart. Say, "Today, we are going to have more fun practicing our visualization skills." Provide students with drawing paper. Read short stories (see below) or give directions for letters, and have students draw pictures of what they visualize.

2. Explain to students that they are going to practice visualizing as you read a book to them. Choose a mentor text to read aloud as students practice visualizing. Do not show students the pictures as you read. Stop after paragraphs with good details, and ask students to close their eyes and visualize the paragraph. Ask students for details about what they *see* in their minds.

3. Conclude with a reminder of what visualizing is and how students can practice this skill.

4. Continue to read other mentor texts and practice making connections.

Cathy's Connections

Providing an anchor chart for students to reference allows them to build independence. Explaining and referring to the chart during multiple lessons provides students with a clear visual for easy connections.

Story 3	Story 4
I am in outer space with my friend. We are astronauts. We see an alien fly over us. There are stars in the sky.	I am one of the three pigs. I am wearing a green shirt. I love mud, but all pigs do; I am also wearing a hat.

Making Predictions—Day 1

Overview

This lesson takes place over two days. Students are asked to understand and use comprehension strategies. Students practice making predictions about what will happen in picture books.

Materials

- *Making Predictions Animal Pictures* (page 246; see Digital Resources for a color version)
- mentor text (*I Went Walking* by Sue Williams is used in this lesson)

Procedure

1. Display the *Making Predictions Animal Pictures.* Say, "Students, before I read the book today, let's look at some pictures and see if we can *predict* what the story is about. *Predicting* means we use what we know to think about what *could* happen. Let's look at these four pictures. What do you think the book could be about?" Wait for responses (the book *could be* about animals in general).

2. Display the cover of *I Went Walking*, and tell students, "Here is the book cover. This book takes place on a farm." Pause and wait for reactions. You want students to react to the crab not being on the farm. Say, "Hmmm, I think you are right. Our prediction about the book being about all animals doesn't work."

3. Continue by saying, "Now that I've told you the setting of the book is on the farm, let's predict what animals we will see in the book." Have students turn to partners and talk about their predictions and why. Provide and model using the sentence frame, *I predict a _____ will be in the book because_____.* Encourage students to make sure their partners are using the frame and not just saying one word. Allow for some think time, and let students share with their partners. Then, call on three students to share aloud. Discuss why students are leaving the crab out of their predictions.

4. Read the book aloud. Each time you come to one of the animal pictures, give students a thumbs-up. When the book is finished, ask if their predictions were correct.

5. Conclude the lesson by saying, "We are practicing predicting this week. Today, we practiced predicting *before* reading a text." Provide clues about the next lesson in your daily schedule by saying something like "Now, I'm going to send you back to your seats. There are counters on your desks. What do you predict we are going do next?" Wait for responses. "Right, let's go do some math."

Cathy's Connections

When reading aloud chapter books, I like to prompt students to use the chapter titles to predict what will happen next.

See the Digital Resources for pieces to make a student-created anchor chart for Making Predictions. See pages 231–234 for a sample lesson on how to build an anchor chart with students.

Making Predictions Animal Pictures

Making Predictions—Day 2

Materials

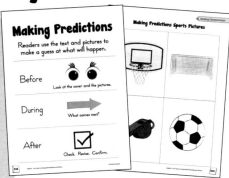

- *Making Predictions* chart (page 248 see Digital Resources for a color version)
- mentor text (*Froggy Plays Soccer* by Jonathan London is used in this lesson)
- *Making Predictions Sports Pictures* (page 249; see Digital Resources for a color version)

Procedure

1. Display the *Making Predictions* chart. Review yesterday's lesson, referencing the chart. Guide students to see that they only made predictions before they read the book yesterday. Say, "Look, there are other times we can make predictions." Discuss the other times when readers can make predictions (*during* and *after* reading). Tell students they will practice that today.

2. Display the cover of *Froggy Plays Soccer*. Refer to the *Making Predictions* chart, and ask, "Who can use the chart to show me what we should do *before* we read this book?" Have a student volunteer come point to the eyes and the words. Say, "Okay, let's look at the cover and a few pictures in the book and predict what will happen." Show students the page with Froggy doing cartwheels, so they might predict he isn't very good at playing soccer.

3. Display the *Making Predictions Sports Pictures*. Ask students to think about the cover of the book and the displayed pictures, and make predictions about what they will see in the book. Say, "I wonder if the net is in the book. Maybe Froggy decides to play basketball. I'm not sure."

4. Read the first half of the book. Ask students if they saw any of the pictures that were displayed.

5. Point to the *Making Predictions* chart, and say, "If we look at our chart, we know we can predict during our reading. We can think about what comes next. Look at our pictures. What do you think will come next?" Allow students to share their predictions. Then, continue reading to the end of the book.

6. At the end of the book, check the predictions. Did Froggy play soccer? (*Yes.*) Did he wear cleats? (*Yes.*) Did he make a goal? (*Yes!*) Did he need a net? (*No.*)

7. Close the lesson by saying, "We are practicing the skills that readers use. We will keep practicing making predictions as we read other books."

Cathy's Connections

There is no need to try and simplify the words *revise* and *confirm*. Students are fully capable of using "big words" if we explain what they mean.

Making predictions is something students do without even knowing they are doing it. Teaching a few strategies for predicting can make this skill permanent.

Making Predictions

Readers use the text and pictures to make a guess at what will happen.

Before

Look at the cover and the pictures.

During

What comes next?

After

Check. Revise. Confirm.

Making Predictions Sports Pictures

Main Idea and Supporting Details—Day 1

Overview

This lesson takes place over three days. Students are asked to understand and use comprehension strategies. Students practice identifying the main idea and supporting details using picture support with short stories.

Materials

- *Identify Main Idea* chart (page 251; see Digital Resources for a color version)
- *Birthday Party Pictures* (page 252; see Digital Resources for a color version)

Procedure

1. Display the *Identify Main Idea* chart. Say "Today, we are going to talk about *main idea* and *supporting details*. Let's talk about those words first. *Main* means the most important. The main idea is the most important part of what we read, and it's what the whole story is about. The supporting details are parts of the story that help or hold up the main idea. Look at our tables. The legs hold up the tabletop. That's what supporting details do, they give details to support the main idea."

2. Discuss the chart with "I like to make my own pizza" being the main idea. The supporting details are: pepperoni, cheese, and onions. Tell students they will practice identifying the main idea and supporting details.

3. Display *Birthday Party Pictures*. Tell students, "If these are the supporting details: *a hat, a cupcake, a balloon,* and *a present,* what do you think the main idea of this story is?" Wait for student responses.

4. Read the *Main Idea Story* on this page. Then say, "Let's check ourselves. Is the whole story about being excited about a birthday party? Then, that's the main idea. *Main idea* is usually a sentence about the topic. The topic of our story would be *birthday party,* so the main idea would be, '*I am so excited for my birthday party*!' Sometimes, we are confused by the difference between topic and main idea. But don't let it confuse you. The topic is one or two words, and the main idea is a whole sentence."

5. Discuss the details provided in the story and how they support or hold up the main idea. Allow students to reference the pictures or reread the story and stop to write the details as you encounter them in the story.

6. Close the lesson by saying, "You did a fantastic job today. You looked at the pictures to determine the main idea. You listened to a story and figured what it was mostly about—a birthday party. We talked about the birthday party, and we talked about details that supported it. You did great work today."

Main Idea Story

I am so excited for my birthday party. I have invited my friends, and everything is ready. My mom made cupcakes, and balloons are tied to the table legs. My friends brought me presents, and they are wearing party hats.

See the Digital Resources for pieces to make a student-created anchor chart for Main Idea and Supporting Details. See pages 231–234 for a sample lesson on how to build an anchor chart with students.

Identify Main Idea

Readers can tell what a text is mostly about.

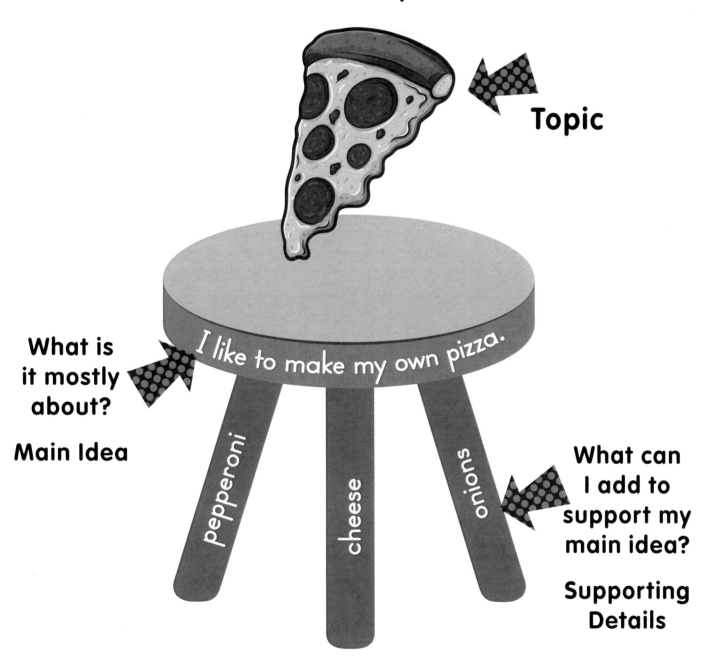

Topic

What is it mostly about?

Main Idea

I like to make my own pizza.

pepperoni

cheese

onions

What can I add to support my main idea?

Supporting Details

Birthday Party Pictures

Main Idea and Supporting Details—Day 2

Materials

- *Identify Main Idea* chart (page 251; see Digital Resources for a color version)
- *Main Idea Wheels* (page 254; see Digital Resources for a color version and additional wheels); copy on card stock, be sure there is one wheel per pair of students
- chart paper

Procedure

1. Call students to the carpet to review the *Identify Main Idea* chart and yesterday's lesson. Then say, "Today, we are going to play a game to practice main idea and supporting details."

2. Assign students partners, and distribute one wheel from *Main Idea Wheels* to each pair. Tell students they will work with their partners to decide on the topic, the main idea (make sure it's a sentence), and the supporting details. Say "Once you are finished, you will find another group and share your wheels. You will tell them your topic, main idea, and supporting details. Then, you will listen to the other group tell about their wheel. If you agree with them, give them a thumbs-up, and move to find another group to share your wheel."

3. Provide time for pairs to work together and for students to share their wheels with other groups.

4. Call students back to the carpet. Review each wheel together with the class. Create a chart to record the wheel number, topic, and main idea for each wheel. Discuss the details.

5. Say, "This is a great chart. We are showing the difference between the topic and main idea, and the wheel shows us the details. Tomorrow, we will write more information on our chart, and we will practice identifying the main idea and supporting details some more."

6. Repeat the activity on other days, rotating the wheels between groups or using different wheels. (See the Digital Resources for additional wheels.)

Talking about main idea and supporting details is important and, at this level, is typically accomplished with pictures and simple written responses. As students develop reading skills, simple paragraphs can be added.

Main Idea Wheels

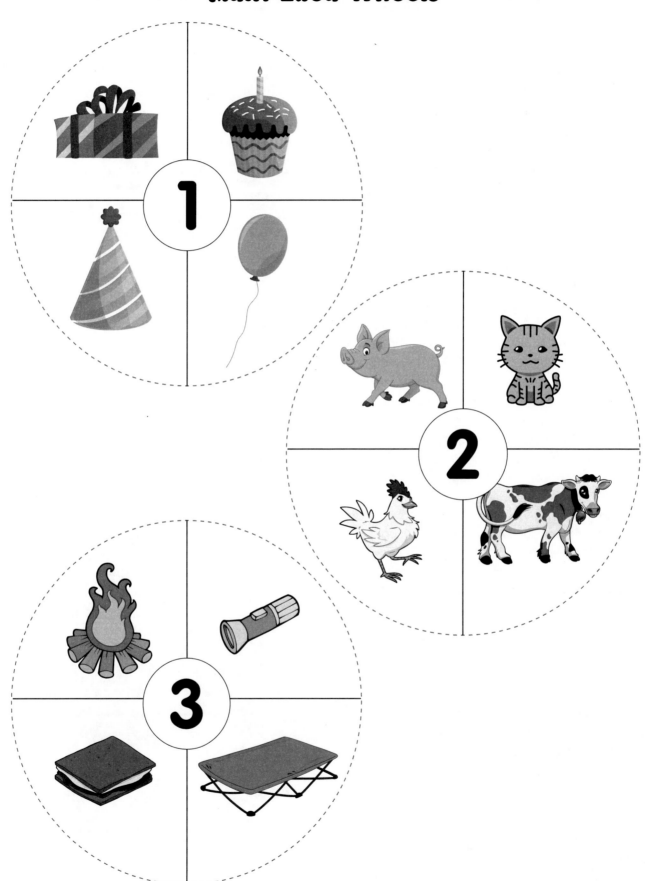

Main Idea and Supporting Details—Day 3

Materials

- *Identify Main Idea* chart (page 251; see Digital Resources for a color version)
- class-created main idea chart from Day 2
- *Ocean Scene* (page 256; see Digital Resources for a color version)
- *Ocean Scene Pictures* (page 257; see Digital Resources for a color version); cut apart

Procedure

1. With students on the carpet, say, "We have been working hard at identifying the main idea and the supporting details. Who can tell me the difference between a topic and a main idea?" (Wait for responses.) Refer to the *Identify Main Idea* chart as needed.

2. Say, "We are going to continue to practice main idea and supporting details." Display *Ocean Scene*. Tell students, "The picture is the main idea. I need help making a main idea sentence." Ask students what the topic is (ocean, sea, beach, etc.). Ask students to help with a main idea sentence (e.g., *I love going to the beach*.). Record the topic and main idea on the chart created in the Day 2 lesson. Ask students to help you write (either interactively or with modeled writing).

3. Ask students to tell you some supporting details for this main idea. Affirm appropriate responses.

4. Show *Ocean Scene Pictures* to students, one at a time. Ask students if the picture could be a supporting detail. Students should be able to say yes (mermaid, turtle, shark, jellyfish) or no (envelope/valentine/mail, acorn).

5. Continue to practice with additional scenes and pictures as needed. (See Digital Resources.)

6. Close the lesson by saying, "Students, I am so proud of your work this week. We have been able to identify the topic and main idea and find supporting details."

Main Idea and Supporting Details Assessments are provided on pages 258–259. Use these to determine if additional practice is needed with this concept.

Ocean Scene

124548—The Road to Independent Reading and Writing

Ocean Scene Pictures

Name _____

Main Idea Assessment 1

Directions: Look at the details. Cut and glue the main idea. Turn your paper over, and write a Main Idea sentence.

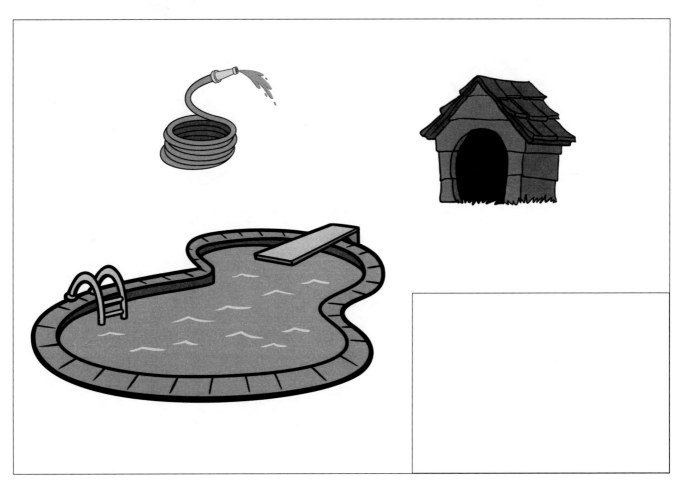

yard   Arctic

Main Idea Assessment 2

Directions: Look at the main idea. Cut and glue three details.

Compare and Contrast—Day 1

Overview

This lesson takes place over four days. Students are asked to understand and use comprehension strategies. Students practice comparing and contrasting by telling how things are alike and different.

Materials

- *Compare and Contrast Pictures* (pages 261–262; see Digital Resources for a color version); cut apart
- *Compare and Contrast* chart (page 263; see Digital Resources for a color version)

Procedure

1. Display the pictures of the dog and fish on *Compare and Contrast Pictures*. Ask students to turn and talk to partners to share what they know about these animals.

2. Gather students' attention and say, "I have been listening to your conversations, and I know you know a lot about these animals." Ask two students to tell you something about a dog and two students to tell you something about a fish.

3. Say, "Today, we aren't going to be talking about just a dog or just a fish, we are going to be talking about a dog and a fish and how they are alike and how they are different. Who has ideas about this?" Call on several students to give examples of how they are alike (animals, pets, small, etc.) and how they are different (fur/scales, legs/fins, lives on land/ lives in water, etc.).

4. Say, "When we *compare*, we tell how things are alike. When we *contrast*, we tell how they are different." Show students the *Compare and Contrast* chart. "This chart can remind us to think about how things are alike and how they are different when we read. Tomorrow, we are going to use this chart to learn more about compare and contrast. You did a great job today."

> See the Digital Resources for pieces to make a student-created anchor chart for Compare and Contrast. See pages 231–234 for a sample lesson on how to build an anchor chart with students.

Compare and Contrast Pictures

dog

fish

Compare and Contrast Pictures *(cont.)*

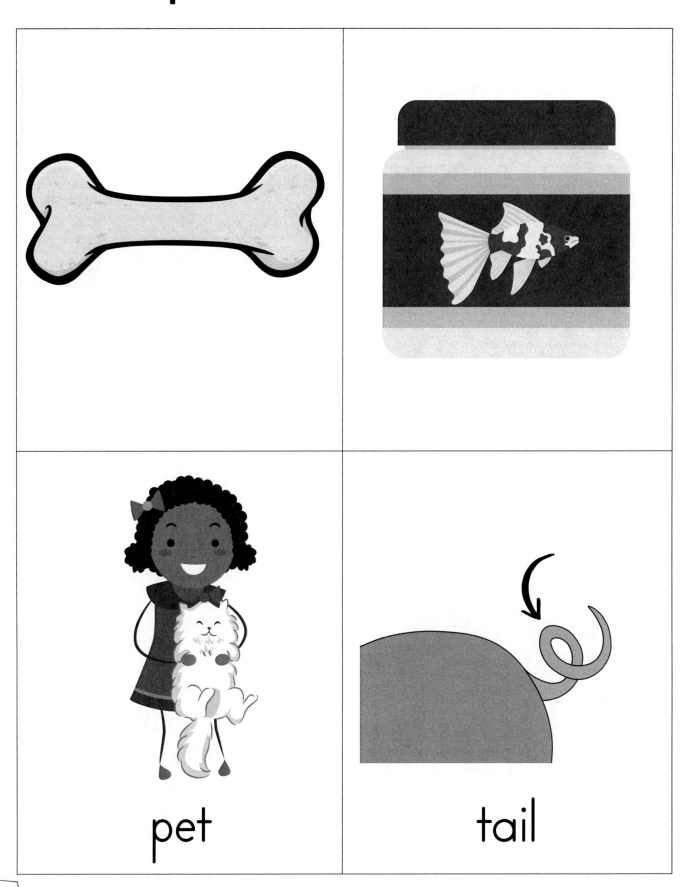

pet

tail

Compare and Contrast

Readers look at how things are alike and different.

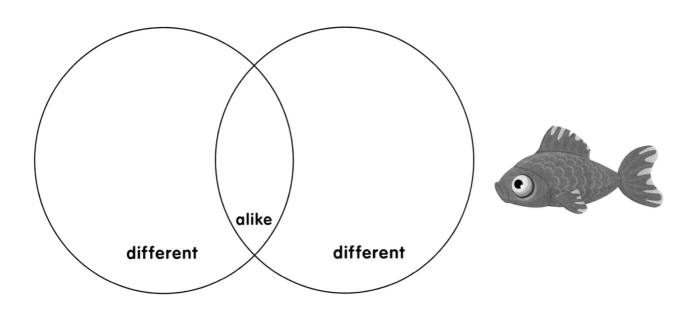

different   alike   different

different	alike	different

Compare and Contrast—Day 2

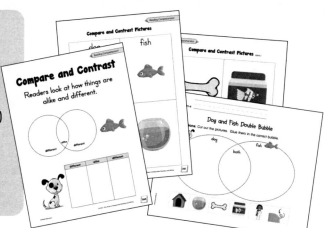

Materials

- *Compare and Contrast* chart (page 263; see Digital Resources for a color version)
- two sheets of chart paper (draw two overlapping circles on one and a three-column chart on the other)
- *Compare and Contrast Pictures* (pages 261–262; see Digital Resources for a color version); cut apart
- student copies of *Dog and Fish Double Bubble* (page 266)

Procedure

1. Call students to the carpet, and review what *compare* and *contrast* mean. If they need reminders, show them the *Compare and Contrast* chart and pictures from yesterday. Say, "Strong readers compare and contrast. They tell how things are alike and how they are different when they read." Yesterday, we talked about the dog and fish and how they are alike and different. Today, we are going to use the two different charts to show how two things are alike and different."

2. Display the chart with the overlapping circles. Tell students, "First, we are going to use a double bubble." Explain that *double* means *two*, and the circles look like bubbles. Say, "One bubble is going to be only about the dog (put the dog picture in one circle), and one bubble is going to be only about the fish (put the fish picture in one circle). See how the bubbles overlap, and there is a space in the middle? That is going to be where we talk about the dog and the fish."

3. Say, "Let's look at one picture at a time and decide where we are going to put it." Take the picture of the doghouse, and ask students which animal this picture is for. Ask a student volunteer to put the doghouse in the bubble with the dog. Show the picture of the bowl. Ask students about this picture, then ask another student to put it in the bubble with the fish.

4. Next, choose the picture labeled *pet*, and say, "This picture says *pet*, do you think I should put it in the dog bubble? They are pets, right? But wait a minute. I think I should put it in the fish bubble because a fish can be a pet." Wait for their reactions. "Oh, I know. I think a dog can be a pet and a fish can be a pet, so it must go in the middle." Continue with the remaining cards, placing them in either the bubbles or the middle section and asking students to put the pictures on the correct space.

Compare and Contrast—Day 2 *(cont.)*

Procedure *(cont.)*

5. Display the three-column chart. Label the first column *Different*, the second column *Alike*, and the third column *Different*. Remove the pictures from the double bubble and display them each one at a time again. Work with students to determine where to place them on the new chart.

6. Say, "Now, you get a chance to make your own chart to compare and contrast a dog and fish." Distribute copies of *Dog and Fish Double Bubble* to students. Allow them time to complete the activity. Monitor students as they work. Save their papers for a writing activity on Day 4.

7. Say, "What a great job telling how the dog and the fish are alike and different. You were able to tell what was only about the dog, what was only about the fish, and what was about both of them. You were able to compare, that means tell how they are alike, and contrast, that means tell how they are different. Tomorrow, we are going to write about these charts. I can't wait."

Learning to compare and contrast is valuable in all content areas, not just reading. See the Digital Resources for additional patterns for repeating this four-day lesson sequence.

Name

Dog and Fish Double Bubble

Directions: Cut out the pictures. Glue them in the correct bubble.

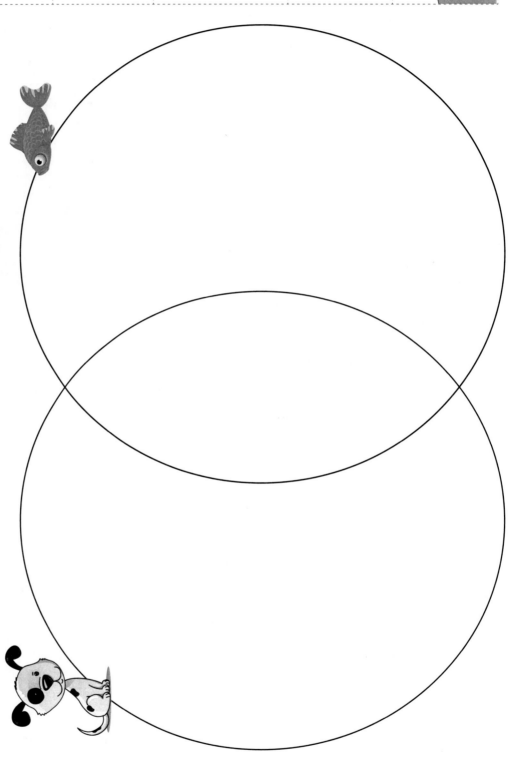

Compare and Contrast—Day 3

Materials

- *Compare and Contrast* chart (page 263; see Digital Resources for a color version)
- double bubble and three-column charts (from Day 2)
- chart paper

Procedure

1. Gather students around the *Compare and Contrast* chart, and review what it tells about being strong readers. Make sure they answer, "Strong readers can compare and contrast, they tell how things are alike and different." Review the compare and contrast charts made yesterday. Say, "Let's review the charts we made yesterday. What is this chart called? (double bubble) What is this chart called? (three-column chart) What do we do with these charts?" (compare and contrast, tell how things are alike and how they are different)

2. Say, "Today, we are going to write a story using our charts. I am so excited to show you how to do this. You'll be doing it by yourself in no time." Display a blank sheet of chart paper. Say, "First, we are going to write our title. Our title will be *Dog and Fish*. Let's write that. We can copy it from our chart." Choose one student to come write *dog*, one student to write *and*, and one student to write *fish*. Make sure you remind students about capitals in titles and spaces.

3. Next say, "The first sentence will be about the dog. Which picture should we talk about today? Should we talk about the bone or the doghouse?" Get a vote from students, and decide which sentence to write. Keep it simple, and lead them to write sight-word heavy sentences, such as *Dogs have a doghouse* or *A dog can have a bone*. Again, invite students to the chart paper to participate in writing the sentence about dogs.

4. When the title and first sentence are finished, ask students to talk about the double bubble and the sentence written. Say, "I am so proud of our writing today. We wrote the title. Who can read it?" Wait for a student response or lead students in reading it. Say, "The first sentence we wrote was about the dog today. Who can read this?" Once again, lead them in reading the sentence.

5. Save all materials, and say, "Tomorrow, we are going to write about the fish. Who can look at our double bubble or three-column chart and tell me something we can write about the fish?" Wait for student responses, and say, "I am looking forward to tomorrow's writing."

Compare and Contrast—Day 4

Materials

- *Compare and Contrast* chart (page 263; see Digital Resources for a color version)
- double bubble and three-column charts (from Day 2)
- writing chart (from Day 3)
- *Dog and Fish Double Bubble* student papers (completed and saved from Day 2)
- student copies of *Dog and Fish Writing* (page 269)

Procedure

1. Gather students on the carpet. Review the *Compare and Contrast* chart and the dog and fish double bubble and three-column charts made on Day 2. Also, take time to reread the title and sentence the class wrote on Day 3.

2. Direct students' attention to the dog and fish charts. Identify fish as the topic of the next sentence. Work with students to follow the procedures from Day 3 to write a sentence about fish. Again, guide students toward a sentence with many words from the word wall, so it can be referenced while writing. For example, *The fish is in the bowl* or *The fish eats fish food.*

3. Explain to students that the last sentence will be about both the dog and fish. Have students help write a sentence about both animals. For example, *The dog and the fish are pets* or *They both have a tail.*

4. Tell students they will have a chance to write their own sentences about comparing dogs and fish. Distribute students' *Dog and Fish Double Bubble* completed on Day 2. Also, distribute *Dog and Fish Writing* to students. Allow them time to write their sentences. As students are working, identify any who need extra support, and either provide them sentence starters or pull them into a small group to work with them to write the sentences.

5. Gather students back on the carpet. Allow several students to share what they wrote. Conclude by saying, "I'm so proud of you and the good writing you did today. You wrote about how a dog and fish were alike and different. Great work!"

Cathy's Connections

Keep anchor charts displayed in the room after you have taught the concept. This allows students to refer to the charts when they are reading and to build independence. Referring to the charts during other lessons provides students with a clear visual for easy connections.

Name _____

Dog and Fish Writing

Dogs and Fish

Summarizing

Overview

Students are asked to understand and use comprehension strategies. Students practice summarizing using a strategy to help them include important parts of a story.

Materials

- *Jack and Jill Picture Cards* (page 272; see Digital Resources for a color version); cut apart
- *Summarize* chart (page 273; see Digital Resources for a color version); cover the answers in the third column with sticky notes
- *Hickory Dickory Dock Picture Cards* (page 274; see Digital Resources for a color version)

Procedure

1. Show students the *Jack and Jill Picture Cards* (withhold picture with the water coming out of the pail). Recite the nursery rhyme. Encourage those who know it to recite it with you. Point to the pictures as you recite the rhyme.

2. Say, "Boys and girls, we are going to practice making a summary of this nursery rhyme. A *summary* is a faster way to tell the whole story. I can turn a whole book into a summary of just a few words. Today, we are going to answer a few questions to make a summary."

3. Display the *Summarize* chart. Say, "When you summarize a story, you tell the important parts. We can use this chart to help us create a summary." Refer to the chart as you ask students the following questions about the nursery rhyme. Remove the sticky notes from the chart as students respond.

   - Who is the story about? (Jack and Jill) Say, "Right, Jack and Jill are the *somebody* in the story."
   - What did Jack and Jill want? (water) Say, "That's right again, they *wanted* a pail of water."
   - What was the problem in the story?" (Jack fell down.) Say, "That will go in the space with *but*. Let's say it from the beginning. Jack and Jill *wanted* a pail of water, *but* Jack fell down."
   - What happened after that? (Jill fell down, too.)

Summarizing *(cont.)*

Procedure *(cont.)*

4. Say, "Good job, let's tell the summary from the beginning. *Jack and Jill wanted* a pail of water, *but* Jack fell down, and *so* did Jill."

5. Say, "Finally, we need to give the ending. Let's look at the *and* part of the chart. *And* what happened at the end—the water fell out of the pail. I know it doesn't say that exactly in the poem, but we know that's what happened." Display the picture of the pail with the water spilling, and remove the sticky note from the chart. Work together to read the whole summary: *Jack and Jill wanted* a pail of water, *but* Jack fell down, *so* did Jill, *and* the water fell out.

6. Practice using the chart by summarizing the nursery rhyme "Hickory Dickory Dock." Display the *Hickory Dickory Dock Picture Cards*. Recite the nursery rhyme. Then, repeat the procedure described above. Practice reciting the entire summary for *Hickory Dickory Dock*.

7. Close by saying, "You are very good at summarizing stories because I know you are strong readers. We'll do more tomorrow."

Cathy's Connections

Summaries are difficult, so repeat the summarizing procedure with different nursery rhymes and classic tales to build students' skills.

See the Digital Resources for pieces to make an anchor chart for Summarizing. See pages 231–234 for a sample lesson on how to build an anchor chart with students.

Jack and Jill Picture Cards

124548—The Road to Independent Reading and Writing

Summarize

Readers use a summary to tell the big moments in a story.

S	Somebody	Jack and Jill
W	wanted	to fetch a pail of water
B	but	Jack fell down
S	so	Jill came tumbling after
A	and	the water spilled.

Hickory Dickory Dock Picture Cards

Making Inferences—Day 1

Overview

This lesson takes place over two days. Students are asked to understand and use comprehension strategies. Students practice making inferences by analyzing smaller pieces.

Materials

- *Making Inferences–Picture 1* (page 276; see Digital Resources for a color version)
- *Making Inferences–Picture 2* (page 277; see Digital Resources for a color version)
- *Making INferences* chart (page 278; see Digital Resources for a color version)

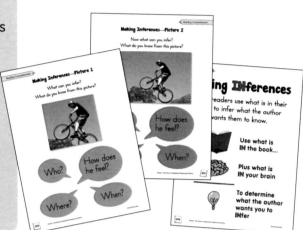

Procedure

1. Display *Making Inferences–Picture 1*. Begin by asking students to describe the picture.

2. Then, ask questions about the picture.
   - *Who* is in the picture? (boy)
   - *What* is he doing? (riding a bike or motorcycle)
   - *How* do you know? (he has on a helmet)
   - *How* does he feel? (he looks like he's concentrating or being careful)

3. Affirm students answers by saying, "Wow! Listen to you. You got all that information from a picture. How did you figure that out?" You want them to understand they can make decisions about what is happening by looking at a picture because of their schema or background knowledge. Say, "You made decisions about what was happening by looking at a picture because you have information in your brain that helps you make those decisions.

4. Say, "Let's look at the full picture." Display *Making Inferences–Picture 2*. Say, "Oh my, I think that's why he is concentrating. He's up so high! But look, you were right. You said he was on a bike or motorcycle, and you said he was concentrating. Great job!"

5. Display the *Making Inferences* chart. Discuss the idea of using what you observe and what you know to figure something out.

6. Conclude the lesson by saying, "Students, today you did an incredible job. You answered some questions in order to help you understand a picture. That is called making inferences. We are going to talk more about that tomorrow. Good job!"

See the Digital Resources for pieces to make a student-created anchor chart for Making Inferences. See pages 11 and 281–285 for sample lessons on how to build an anchor chart with students.

Making Inferences—Picture 1

What can you infer?
What do you know from this picture?

Who?

How does he feel?

Where?

When?

Making Inferences—Picture 2

Now what can you infer?
What do you know from this picture?

Who?

How does he feel?

Where?

When?

Making INferences

Readers use what is in their brains to infer what the author wants them to know.

Use what is IN the book...

+

Plus what is IN your brain

To determine what the author wants you to INfer

Making Inferences—Day 2

Overview

Students are asked to understand and use comprehension strategies. Students practice making inferences by analyzing smaller pieces.

Materials

- *Making Inferences* chart (page 278; see Digital Resources for a color version)
- *Sea Animals Inferences* (page 280; see Digital Resources for a color version)

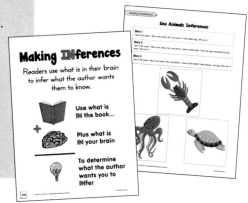

Procedure

1. Gather students on the carpet. Display the *Making Inferences* chart. Review yesterday's lesson by having students recall some of the inferences they made about the biker. Explain to students they will practice making inferences today, too.

2. Display only the pictures from *Sea Animal Inferences*. Allow students to share what they know about the three pictures. Say, "We know that because we used our brains to help us. Now, we are going to use some words to help us, too."

3. Say, "I want you to listen to this story." Read *Story 1*. Say, "What animal am I talking about?" Allow students to share their responses. Say, "How do you know I'm talking about the octopus?" Wait for student responses, but most will say the octopus has eight legs. Make sure to count the legs in the picture to double-check.

4. Continue by saying, "We used our brains to help us understand the pictures and the words to help us understand exactly what picture we were talking about. Let's do it again." Repeat by reading the other two stories and identifying the correct animals, asking students to explain their understandings.

5. Conclude the lesson by saying, "Students, today you did an incredible job! You used your brains and you used the words to understand the story. Wonderful work!"

See the Digital Resources for additional stories and pictures for more practice with this activity.

Sea Animals Inferences

Story 1

I live in the ocean. I like to eat crabs, fish, and clams. I have eight legs. Who am I?

Story 2

I live in the ocean. I like to eat crabs, fish, and clams. I have a hard shell. I have ten legs, including two big claws. Who am I?

Story 3

I live in the ocean. I like to eat crabs, fish, and plants. I have a hard shell. I have flippers, not legs. Who am I?

124548—The Road to Independent Reading And Writing

Vocabulary Strategies

One of the key elements to reading comprehension is vocabulary. If you think of all the layers of comprehension like building a road, you need to think of vocabulary building like filling the potholes in the road. If vocabulary knowledge is incomplete, the road to comprehension will be bumpy. Using an anchor chart as a road map can create a smooth ride for vocabulary. This section contains a variety of strategies for building vocabulary anchor charts.

Diagrams

Diagrams are simply labeled pictures. Building a diagram is especially good for nonfiction texts. You can draw a quick image for use in making diagrams or find images online. Use sentence strips or index cards as the labels. Allow students to attach the labels to the picture. When students help build a diagram, they are more likely to use it in writing or independent practice.

Vocabulary Maps

Vocabulary maps provide a structure for students to collaborate and show what they understand about vocabulary before direct instruction. Label sheets of construction paper with each of the following five categories: characters, setting, things/nouns, verbs/action words, and new to me. Write the vocabulary words selected for the book on sticky notes. The following is an example of words that can be selected for *Pirates Past Noon* by Mary Pope Osborn.

Characters: Jack, Annie, Morgan, Captain Bones, Pinky and Stinky

Setting: treehouse, pirate ship, island, Frog Creek

Nouns: chest, medallion, treasure map, thunderstorm, whale's eye, rock

Verbs: running, growled, rowing, pulling, read, dig

New to Us: gale, vile, clutched, raid

Distribute sticky notes to students. Allow student pairs to discuss their words and then stick them in the correct category. Review each sticky note with the class to determine if it is placed in the correct category and then provide direct instruction on each word in the "New to Us" category. Place the categories on a larger sheet of chart paper so they are in one place. For added interest, the chart paper can be shaped to reflect the story. For example: a pirate map for *Pirates Past Noon*, a doghouse for Clifford books by Norman Bridwell, or a nest for *Stellaluna* by Janelle Cannon.

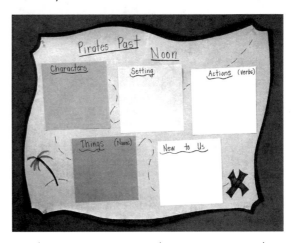

Book: *Pirates Past Noon* by Mary Pope Osborn

Vocabulary Strategies (cont.)

Concept Muraling

Murals, by definition, are large pictures painted directly on a wall. In the classroom, murals are not painted directly on the wall, but they are large pictures affixed to the wall. A mural should be created in front of students or with students. Murals can be added to as needed. Many lessons can be combined on one mural.

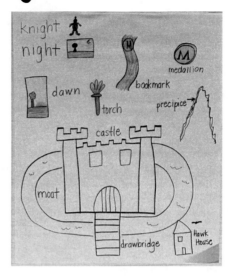

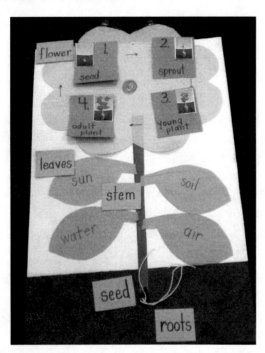

Plant Mural

The plant mural was created with modeled writing over a period of three weeks. After a whole-group lesson, students created their own murals. The first week, parts of a plant were created by adding one part per day. On Monday, the mural contained just brown soil. A seed was added (either a paper seed as in this picture or an actual sunflower seed) and labeled. On Tuesday, the roots (yarn) were glued to the seed and labeled. On Wednesday, the stem was added from the seed up the paper and labeled. On Thursday, the leaves were added and labeled. On Friday, the petals/flower were added and labeled. The second week, the lessons were about what a plant needs to grow (sun, water, soil, and air). The third and final week, the lessons were about the life cycle of a plant. The life cycle was added to the flower.

Castle Mural

For the castle mural, the vocabulary was built with students at the carpet. The pictures were quickly drawn to prepare students for some of the vocabulary. Not all words are introduced before they are read. Some words are added as they are found in the text.

Frayer Model

Created by Dorothy Frayer and her colleagues at the University of Wisconsin, the Frayer Model uses likes and differences to define a word. Students are asked to determine the definition, characteristics of the words, examples of the word, and non-examples. A suggestion is to use a Frayer Model with one word per week. This word could be a word from any discipline: reading, writing, math, science, or social studies. Each week a word is introduced, and one section of the Frayer Model is added. On Monday, the word is introduced, and a clear definition is provided. On Tuesday, discuss the characteristics or facts about the word. On Wednesday, share examples of the word. On Thursday, share non-examples. The following week, students can create their own Frayer Model in a vocabulary center. After creating their Frayer Model, students can use the information in the model to write about the word.

Vocabulary Strategies *(cont.)*

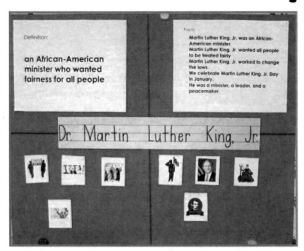

Text Gradients

Sometimes called semantic gradients or vocabulary gradients, the meaning is the same. A gradient is an inclined part of a road or embankment. With a text gradient, we start with a word, and as it moves through a gradient, the nuances of the word are explored. Students building their vocabulary can move from all things being *big* or *little* to some things are *big*, *large*, *huge*, or *giant*, or they are *little*, *small*, *tiny*, or *miniscule*. As a whole-group lesson, students are asked to take a list of words and rank them from a starting point and move the vocabulary along a continuum for a more specific use of the word. Students discovering the gradations in text can lead to a better understanding of the word.

Students can also discover gradients already existing in text. Using a mentor book, students can listen for the gradients of the word *said* in the text. By drawing your attention to these gradients in text, students can use the more specific words in their writing.

Cathy's Connections

I love paint chips! To make using text gradients fun, supply your students with gradients written on paint chips. Students writing in journals or in centers can pick paint chips and incorporate a gradient in their writing.

Vocabulary Strategies (cont.)

List, Group, Label

Exactly as the title suggests, we are going to list, group, and label vocabulary. Student groups are given a list of words with no extra information. Younger students may need pictures for the words to create a student-driven lesson. Students must read the words and decide how they should be grouped and how these groups should be labeled. Teachers can use these groups and labels to know what their students have in their arsenal of vocabulary. Some student groups may only be able to look at the size of the items or where to find the items, while some student groups will be able to look at the objects' functions or needs. The value in this lesson is as much about vocabulary as it is about discussion among students.

In Our Classroom		
1. school	7. bookbag	13. paper
2. bus	8. crayons	14. music
3. mailbox	9. snack	15. rug
4. chair	10. pencil	16. desk
5. nametags	11. computer	17. table
6. hall	12. lunch box	18. books

Act It Out

Get up and get moving. Students who are able to move and interact with language will make a newer and deeper connection. In *Knights At Dawn* by Mary Pope Osborn, there is a moment when Jack is hanging from a precipice. Knowing students would not know what a *precipice* was, they also would not know how Jack felt hanging from it. There would be no connection. So, for this vocabulary word, consider moving the lesson outside the classroom to the playground. Explain that a *precipice* is a cliff or a ledge. Stand at the edge of a piece of playground equipment that is raised off the ground with your arms spread and yell, "I am at a precipice!" Then, jump off the equipment. Allow students to come stand at the precipice and jump, too. A way to further act out precipice is to hang from the edge of a piece of playground equipment to show students "hanging from the precipice." Allow students to do the same. This helps make the word real. When you get to the point in the book when Jack is hanging from the precipice, students will know exactly what it means and will also know how Jack must be feeling.

Vocabulary Strategies *(cont.)*

Journals

Journals can be a powerful tool for vocabulary. As students use new vocabulary words in authentic writing, the meaning is far more real. When students write about something, they etch the meaning in their schema. This doesn't mean you need a vocabulary notebook.

When students are asked to authentically write about the vocabulary words, we are asking them to use what they know and what they learned, and put it in their own words to become part of their vocabularies.

Years ago, when I first taught vocabulary, the weekly assignment was to write the word, write the definition, write the page number from the story, and write the sentence from the story that included the new word. EEK! This actually had no value in adding the vocabulary to the child's schema… it was a handwriting lesson in finding a word and copying the sentence.

I suggest having a vocabulary notebook that allows for definitions or multiple definitions and illustrations and writing original sentences. We can also add sections for synonyms, antonyms, alternate definitions, or just "more understanding" of the word.

Small-Group Instructional Routine

Small group reading, as the name implies, is the process of working with students through the routines and rigor of reading in a small group. Teachers work with students according to their needs on lessons in phonological awareness, phonics, fluency, vocabulary, and comprehension.

A lesson plan lasts 15–30 minutes and contains the following parts:

1. **Warm Read:** (2–3 minutes) Each lesson opens with the teacher choosing a student to read a text from the previous lesson (the warm read). As the student reads, the teacher monitors the student's accuracy and fluency. This helps determine accurate placements, books, and future lessons. The student does not need to read the entire text. The teacher can choose a starting place for the assessment to begin. The other students in the group are rereading other previous texts for decoding, fluency, and comprehension, but should not be reading the same text as the students being evaluated.

2. **Vocabulary:** (2–3 minutes) Vocabulary words are an integral part of the lesson. Students need to be introduced to one or two new words, and they need to review a few sight words during the lesson. Helping them understand new words they may encounter will assist them with comprehension of the text.

3. **New Text:** (2 minutes) Students are introduced to a new book. This introduction is quick, with one or two sentences about the book and one or two quick searches for new or unknown vocabulary words. It is not necessary to "walk" through each page of the book and pre-teach all the words and concepts. Students need to "put in the work" to read without the teacher doing too much. It is vitally important for students to be exposed to text daily. Ideally, a new text should be provided at each group meeting.

4. **Read, Read, Read:** (5 minutes) Students need time to read the text. Ideally, emergent readers need to read through the entire text. Students should be doing the work of reading the entire book themselves, not relying on other students in the group to read parts of the book for them. The effects of round-robin reading, popcorn reading, turn reading, or whatever it could be called, are devastating.

5. **Strategy Practice:** (2–3 minutes) When students are done reading, it is important to practice strategies for areas of reading in which they need additional practice. A list of strategies that can be practiced in a small group setting is provided on pages 290–295. Target these strategies to students' needs based on assessments and observation.

6. **Comprehension:** (2–3 minutes) Books at the kindergarten level contain sight words, decodable text, and repetitive text, so the comprehension levels are typically at the knowledge level. However, making sure students can identify the story elements (when possible), sequence of events, and details is critical. Also, an early introduction to character feelings is important. Relating to a topic makes the story personal and more meaningful for emergent readers.

7. **Word Work/Writing:** (3–4 minutes) Beginning readers should follow up their reading with word work and writing. This could include making words by rearranging letters, doing word sorts, and even writing short responses. Although this seems to be the easiest part of the lesson to skip if time is running out, making time for this as many days as possible is important to providing a well-rounded lesson. Writing can be interactive, dictated, or independent.

Small-Group Instructional Tools

During small-group reading instruction, students should be engaged and actively participating in the lesson. The following is a list of some of tools that can be useful to make this possible:

1. **Magnet Letters**—These are perfect for word work for early readers. Manipulating letters helps all students, especially kinesthetic learners. Changing the vowel in *bad* to make *bed* helps the student understand the consonants remain, but the vowel is changed. Only put out the magnets students will need for the lesson.

2. **Strategy Cards**—Once you've introduced a decoding or other reading strategy, having a few cards for quick review can make the strategy permanent. Give a few cards to each student to help them practice independently while you monitor.

3. **Whisper Phone**—Most students love these! They enable students to hear themselves as they read. Some students need the whisper phone to ensure they are whispering. Some students need it to block out other voices. Some students don't like it at all, so don't force them to use them.

4. **Dry-Erase Boards**—Students should each have an individual dry-erase board available to them as they work with words during the lesson. These can be purchased or made by inserting a sheet of card stock into a sheet protector. I like to have one side with lines for writing and one side blank. (See the Digital Resources for a *Dry-erase Board Template*.)

5. **Dry-Erase Markers**—The markers that are the same width as a pencil and have an eraser on the lid are great for young children to work with because they reinforce a good pencil grip. Make sure the markers are bullet tip. Early writers have trouble with a beveled edge marker.

6. **Spacer/Pointer**—Using a spacer for all writing helps remind students that words need spaces between them. Finding a spacer that can also be used as a pointer will help students track and help ease their finger-pointing necessity.

Instead of purchasing spacers for writing, make your own. Or you can find someone to make them for you. I had a parent who couldn't volunteer in my classroom but wanted to contribute. Once a month, she would hot glue mini-erasers on tongue depressors and write my students' names on them. My students loved these personalized spacers. We used them as both spacers and pointers.

Cathy's Connections

I like to place all the tools students will need in a little container or basket so that each student has all their own supplies. It helps define whose supplies are whose and makes it easier to manage when students have all the supplies they need for the lesson in one place.

Reading Records

Reading records are the record of student oral reading. The teacher listens to the student read while recording accuracy and fluency. They are useful for teachers to get an accurate picture of what students are capable of when reading on their own. Often during lessons, teachers are tempted to jump in during a student's reading of a text to teach or make a point to help the student. When doing a reading record, the situation is set up so that both the teacher and student know it is about an unassisted reading.

There are two types of reading records used during the school year. First, there is a summative assessment called a *cold read*. It is just as implied; students are reading it for the first time. This is a summative assessment because the teacher is able to detect how much students know based on the reading of the text. There are many types of screeners available. The second type of reading record is formative. These records are used with familiar text so the teacher can form the lessons based on students' needs. Typically, the teacher has the text the student is reading on a recording sheet. A check mark is placed above the words students read correctly and any words read incorrectly are marked as well.

Recording the Reading

When a student is reading, three things can occur:

- **Accurate reading:** The student reads the word correctly; you record a check above the text (in a benchmark) or in line with read text (in a formative assessment).
- **Self-correction:** The student misreads the text, then without outside prompting, corrects the error accurately and continues to read with comprehension intact.
- **Errored reading:** The student reads the word incorrectly. They may realize the word is incorrect, as meaning is distorted, but they don't correct it and continue reading or read incorrectly without pause.

Types of Errors

- **Substitution** is the most common type of error, simply replacing the correct word with another word. The teacher writes the substituted word. Each time a word is substituted, it is an error except when dealing with proper names. If a student replaces a proper name, it is only counted as an error once. After that, the error is recorded, but it is not counted. To make the distinction between the proper noun substitution and other substitutions, I write an *N* above the intended word. By writing the *N*, I know it's an error, but it isn't counted in my accuracy percentage.

- **Insertion** is an error that has the student adding words where they don't exist.

- **Omissions** are exactly that: the student omits a word when reading. Some of the time, if the omitted word is an adjective, comprehension may not be distorted.

- **Appeals**, as the title implies, are when a student appeals to the tester for an unknown word.

- **Tolds** are when the tester supplies the word for the reader. This is a slippery slope in the world of reading records. The goal of reading is allowing the reader to decode the text so they can make meaning of the text. If the tester "gives" the word to students, they have not done the work of reading.

Other Reading Codes

- **Self-correction** is, in fact, an error first and a correction second. The error does not count negatively in the accuracy percentage, but the error is analyzed before the self-correction is analyzed. However, the self-correction IS NOT recorded as an error, it is recorded as correct.

- **Repetition** is when a reader rereads a word, phrase, or sentence in the natural progression of the text. This can be a method for the reader to keep the meaning, but it could be a habit that will need to be broken. Too many repetitions can stall comprehension.

Reading Records *(cont.)*

Fluency

Fluency is a part of most universal screening tools. Fluency is usually calculated as words read per minute. Some screeners time students' entire reading and then divide to find the words read per minute. Other screeners only time for the first minute of a student's read and count the number of words read during the first minute. Although you will need to use a stopwatch or clock when the student is reading to calculate a fluency rate, it is not recommended that the student see that you are doing so. It adds to students' anxiety to know they are being timed.

Comprehension

Because reading is about getting to the meaning of the text, comprehension is an important part of a screening tool. Some screening tools first ask students to retell what they have read in their own words. The teacher records everything they say in the recounting of the text. Exactly what the student says is recorded and then the number of words is added up. The number of words used for the retell is compared each time a reading record is done. The goal is to have students increase the number of words they use in their retellings, which shows an increased comprehension of the text as well as an increase in various strategies, such as making inferences and drawing on prior knowledge.

Questions asked to students are another method of testing comprehension. If you are using a universal screener, the questions are usually provided and cover a range of question types from basic recall to inference. If you are creating your own questions, you will want to ask a wide range of types of questions.

Results from the reading, fluency, and comprehension aspects of a reading record should be used to help you make plans for individual students as well as to be able to flexibly place students who are in need of similar lessons in small groups.

Where Does It Go from Here?

When the reading record has been completed, the teacher now has a picture of what the student can read independently and knows where to focus attention.

Strategy Practice

Target small groups of students to practice particular strategies based on their needs. Provided is a list of strategies, a short description, and references to the Digital Resources for additional pages of practice. Copies of the additional pages can be made for each student like an activity sheet, or consider copying enough for a small group and laminating the sheets or placing the copies in sheet protectors. Then, students can use dry-erase markers to complete the activity. Most of the activities are quick and do not require students having their own copies of the activity to take home.

Phonological Awareness

Any of the activities in the Phonological Awareness section (pages 125–131) of this book can be used as small-group mini lessons. Phonological awareness activities work best when targeted to student needs. When used in a small group, the teacher is more easily able to monitor student responses.

Counting Syllables

Identifying syllables helps students hear segments of words and will help with decoding strategies in multisyllabic words later. Emergent and early readers can also be taught the connection between vowels and syllables. Use the *Syllable Picture Cards* (see Digital Resources) to have students name the picture, count the

syllables, and then circle the number of syllables. Students at the earliest level can detect the number of syllables in a given word.

Phonics

Any of the activities in the Phonics section (pages 132–207) of this book can be used as small-group mini lessons. Phonics activities work best when targeted to student needs. When used in a small group, the teacher is more easily able to monitor student responses.

What Would You Expect?

This activity is great practice for students who are not using the letters to guide them when reading. Using the *What Would You Expect? Cards* (see Digital Resources), students look at the position of a shaded box and determine what they would hear at the beginning, middle, and end of the word. The middle sound could be

a vowel sound or could be a consonant sound in a two-syllable word, such as the *d* in the middle of *ladder*.

Strategy Practice *(cont.)*

Flip the Vowel

Vowels can be especially hard for early readers, so repetitive practice is important. Practice long and short vowels using the *Flip the Vowel Cards* (see Digital Resources). These cards contain pictures of a short vowel word and a long vowel

companion. That is, when a student decodes the short vowel word to represent the picture (*pin*), they can add a final *e* to create a long vowel word (*pine*). Students learn that a CVC word with one vowel should be a short vowel, while a word with the final *e* should be a long vowel. Having students write the two words with dry-erase markers and then create oral sentences for both will solidify vowel knowledge.

Same Beginning Sound

The *Same Beginning Sound Cards* (see Digital Resources) use a known sight word as an anchor and have students find the picture that starts the same. Students can put a coin on the correct answer or circle the correct answer with a dry-erase marker.

Find the Vowel, Find the Rime

When early readers are learning to decode unknown words, locating vowels enables them to make decisions about the vowel (one vowel is *usually* short and two vowels are *usually* long). Starting with single rimes, students can build on words with more than one word part. For example, finding the initial rime *ut* in

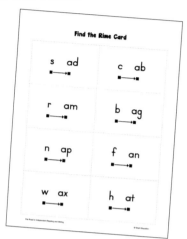

stutter helps students build the potentially unknown word by adding a beginning blend and an ending. Eventually, using early understandings with vowels, students can connect more complex vowel patterns relating to syllables. Have students practice finding the vowel and then identifying the rime. Then, have students go back and add the beginning sound. *Find the Rime Cards* (see Digital Resources) help students practice this strategy for short vowel words. Once students are proficient with short vowel words, build to longer words and long vowel words. This strategy is particularly effective for that small number of students who have trouble blending sounds from the beginning to the end of the word.

Strategy Practice *(cont.)*

Use the Rime

Identifying the rime in a word can be useful for both reading and spelling. Use the *Use the Rime Cards* (see Digital Resources for additional cards) to practice taking a known to create an unknown. The cards provide the anchor picture (e.g., *clap*) and ask the students to use the known rime

to create new words (e.g., *nap, map, zap,* and *cap*). Being able to manipulate the letters and parts of the words helps students develop skills to manipulate sounds in reading and writing.

Get Your Lips Ready

Use the *Get Your Lips Ready Cards* (see Digital Resources) to help students practice getting ready to say a sound when they see a letter. Begin with the cards that contain only the lips with a letter. Display a card, and have students put their lips and mouths in the positions they need

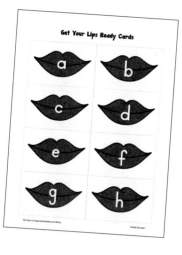

to be in to make the sound. Have students hold their lips in that position until you say, "Sound." At the signal, have students produce the sound. Students should get to a point of automatically getting their lips ready, which will translate to readiness when reading, too. Once students are skilled with that activity, progress to cards that have the lips along with two picture choices at the bottom of the card. Once students get their lips ready with the sound for the letter on the card, they choose which picture

begins with the sound they are ready to say using the *Get Your Lips Ready Cards with Pictures* (see Digital Resources).

Chop the Ending

Students are often intimidated by longer words, so teaching strategies such as Chop the Ending can be useful in helping students tackle these words. Teach students various endings that words can have (i.e., *s, ing,* and *ed*). Then, demonstrate for students how to

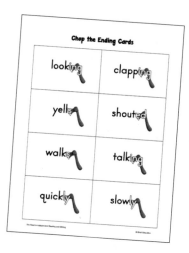

"chop" the ending off the word, leaving a base word that they may recognize or decode if they don't know it. Be sure to model and have students practice adding the endings back onto the base words to read the entire word after they have used the strategy. A list of endings and *Chop the Ending Cards* with endings is provided in the Digital Resources.

Fluency
Text Signals

Punctuation is first introduced as the end mark during whole-group lessons and read-alouds. It should be explained and practiced in more detail in small group lessons. Use the *Sentence Cards* (see Digital Resources) to practice reading the same

sentence using different ending punctuation. This helps students read with expression and understand

Strategy Practice *(cont.)*

how punctuation can help with comprehending the story. The sentence *Look at the big dog.* is a statement of fact. But if the punctuation is changed to a question mark, the student asks the question and wonders if the dog is truly big or big by comparison to something else. Finally, if the same sentence is read with an exclamation mark, then students understand the excitement or fear in the sentence. This is such a fun activity to do as a whole group or as an interactive lesson with students reading with expression or acting out the sentence.

Confused Words

Students often confuse words such as *was* and *saw.* Being able to identify those words quickly helps students with fluent reading. This skill is so important, easy to practice, and it's fun, too. This can be practiced in a small group setting or as an independent intervention. Provide each student with a *Word Fluency Card* (see Digital Resources). Each student roles a number cube and then reads the column with the corresponding number. Students do not compete against one another, but they can compete against themselves. A teacher or interventionist can set a timer and let students read the list, without errors, and time themselves. Each day, they could try to "beat" their own time.

Vocabulary

Any of the activities in the Vocabulary Strategies section (pages 281–285) of this book can be used as a small group mini lesson. Vocabulary activities work best when targeted to student needs. When used in a small group, the teacher is more easily able to monitor student responses.

Semantic Gradients

Semantic gradients help build vocabulary. Students learn vocabulary related to the distinctions of words in a category (e.g., *small* and *tiny*). The *Semantic Gradient Cards* (see Digital Resources) can be used to have students match the vocabulary gradient with the picture. Students can

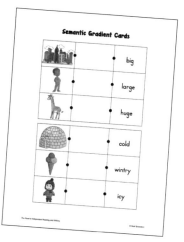

understand an adult can be *big* as compared to themselves, but the giraffe is *large,* and the tallest skyscraper is *huge.* These vocabulary nuances are important when building comprehension.

Strategy Practice (cont.)

Identifying Synonyms

Students should have an awareness of synonyms, even if they don't know that's what they are. For example, if the story is about

a ladybug, they may describe the ladybug as *small*, but also know it's *tiny*. Knowing the ladybug could be small or tiny will help with comprehension. The *Find the Synonym Cards* (see Digital Resources) help students understand there is more than one word to describe something that is small. Have students circle words that mean the same or nearly the same as each other. Have students draw an *X* on the word that does not describe the picture.

Comprehension

Any of the activities in the Reading Comprehension section (pages 229–280) of this book can be used as a small-group mini lesson. Comprehension activities work best when targeted to student needs. When used in a small group, the teacher is more easily able to monitor student responses.

Activate Prior Knowledge

Practice activating prior knowledge by having students describe a picture. Provide students with *Predicting Picture Cards* (see Digital Resources). Have students describe the large picture. Then, have students identify

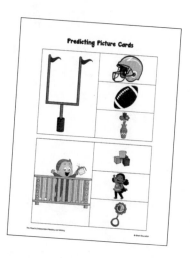

which two smaller pictures go best with the large picture. Have them explain their reasoning. Allow students to share any experiences they have had with the scene or situation.

Build Prior Knowledge

Provide students with a *Building Prior Knowledge Map* (see Digital Resources). The circle in the middle has a title and a picture clue. Either provide a copy to students in the small group and have them cut out the picture cards and glue them around the circle, or laminate the map and have students draw lines

from the pictures on the side to the picture in the circle with a dry-erase marker. Discuss with students which of the pictures provided are details related to the topic in the circle map. The discussion helps build background knowledge about the topic of the text they will read. These circle maps can also be used as maps for independent writing. This activity works especially well when using nonfiction texts.

Make Connections

When students can make connections to text, comprehension is more easily attained. Using the *Making Connection Cards* (see Digital Resources) helps students make connections and use what they know to understand the text. If they see a picture of a hockey player and they can make a connection between the hockey player in the

Strategy Practice *(cont.)*

picture and watching a hockey game on television, then they can understand a little better that most of the story will be on the ice and could have a goalie and a net. Students can often make more than one connection to a topic, but having a conversation about it helps solidify the information.

What Can It Be?

This activity is an oral activity to help with predicting and drawing conclusions as well as inferences. There are no cards for students. It's a type of *I Spy* game. The teacher places an object in a box and then provides clues to students so they can guess what is inside. To do this activity, students must use what they know to accurately predict the object in the box. These types of games help students who are reading predict what is likely to happen next.

Sequencing Activities

Knowing the sequence of events helps students determine what they are reading about. They also help students retell what they have read in  the correct order, too. Use the *Sequencing Cards* (see Digital Resources) to help students practice the correct order of events before reading a text as prediction and after for retelling purposes. Have students indicate the order of the events by writing *1*, *2*, and *3* under the corresponding picture. Have students explain their thinking.

Digital Resources

Accessing the Digital Resources

The digital resources can be downloaded by following these steps:

1. Go to **www.tcmpub.com/digital**

2. Enter the ISBN, which is located on the back cover of the book, into the appropriate field on the website.

3. Respond to the prompts using the book to view your account and available digital content.

4. Choose the digital resources you would like to download. You can download all the files at once, or you can download a specific group of files.

Please note: Some files provided for download have large file sizes. Download times for these larger files will vary based on your download speed.

**ISBN:
9781087631509**

Contents of the Digital Resources

You'll find a wealth of resources that will give you greater flexibility and accessibility than the print resources alone.

- There are color versions of the posters, picture cards, charts, and activity sheets in this book—90+ pages! This allows you to print them in color, and more readily engage young learners.

- An additional 150 pages of teaching materials and student activity sheets are provided (in color) to extend the lessons in the book, giving you everything you need to support student learning.

- The digital versions of the materials are handy for use on interactive whiteboards or for virtual sessions.

- Digital versions of the lesson plans give you increased flexibility in lesson preparation.